THE COMMUNICATIONS AUDIT

The Communications Audit

A guide for managers

Anthony Booth

Gower

658.45
B00.

Published by
Gower Publishing Company Limited,
Gower House,
Croft Road,
Aldershot,
Hants GU11 3HR,
England

The opinions expressed in this book are those of the author and not necessarily those of the British Library.

British Library Cataloguing in Publication Data

Booth, Anthony
    The communications audit: a guide for managers.
    1. Communication in management—Great Britain
    2. Communication in organizations—Great Britain
    I. Title
    658.4'5'0941   HD30.3

ISBN 0–566–02725–9

Printed in Great Britain at the University Press, Cambridge

22. 9. 89.

Contents

Preface

This book was written as a consequence of some research carried out by the author for the Primary Communications Research Centre at the University of Leicester. The research project brief was to examine the status of communications auditing in the UK in the mid 1980s. One of the findings of the project was that whilst many larger organizations in the UK and abroad were commissioning communications audits in order to increase their efficiency, there were a large number of organizations which had not even heard of communications auditing. One of the chief objectives of this book is to begin to fill that information gap and to increase general awareness of the potential value of the communications audit as a management tool.

Anthony Booth

Acknowledgements

I would like to acknowledge my gratitude to all those who helped in the preparation of this work. In particular: to my colleagues at PCRC who happily let me try out various communications auditing techniques on them; to Mary Feeney and Mark Goodwin for their technical inputs; to Richard Heeks and my students on an Open University systems summer school at York in August 1986 for help in conceptual development; to Kate Waters for transforming the handwritten manuscript to the endproduct.

Funding for the project was provided by British Library Research and Development.

AB

Introduction

A communications audit is an activity which involves the measurement and analysis of communications within an organization. There are many different reasons why an organization might wish to audit its communications and a variety of techniques are available to do so. This book will help you decide when you need to look at the communications within your company and will tell you how to begin doing this either internally, or with the aid of outside expertise. This book will not tell you how to communicate; there are literally hundreds of publications in management and other fields that attempt to do this already. Instead, the orientation will be towards the identification of communications problems, and the generation of logical cost-effective solutions to these problems. Large firms, such as those listed in the *Times Top 1000*, are increasingly using the communications audit as a tool to keep their competitive edge, frequently with the aid of management or communications consultants. It is hoped that this publication will help managers in small or medium-sized firms to consider effectively some of the critical decisions that will need to be made about the communications systems in their own firms.

It is frequently tempting to assume that our own communications systems have worked well in the past and so will work well in the future. However, two particular types of change, which are occurring more rapidly at present than previously, make this a dangerous assumption.

The first relates to the changes in the economic environment that have become apparent since the early 1970s; typically the environment has been described as more 'turbulent' than previously. The consequence has been that almost all organizations have had to adapt 'organically' to such changes to some extent, or risk corporate collapse. In many cases company restructuring has been substantial; there is a danger that the communications procedures which were appropriate a few years ago have now become out of step with the changed organization.

The second type of change relates to the rapid technological developments that have occurred, and continue to occur, in the means we use to communicate. For example, normal telephone exchanges are rapidly being replaced by 'intelligent' PABXs (Private Automatic Branch Exchanges), and the use of electronic mail is expanding rapidly. Companies, therefore, need to be able to make decisions concerning the value of such innovations for their own *needs*. Even when faced with the relatively simple decision to install a new PABX, there is a large choice, both of systems and of manufacturers. Also to be considered is the question of whether to carry out the change immediately, or to wait another year because of predicted price or technological breakthroughs in the equipment available.

The difficulty with suggesting 'best buys' of hardware in this book is that some of the advice given would be out of date before publication. We shall, however, look at the broader options available so as to aid decision making by the manager who is not an expert in communications equipment. Our discussion will therefore include sources of up-to-date information, such as monthly journals or magazines concerned with what is available, as well as advising when (and how) it is sensible to bring in a specialist in the field.

The variety of problems that might call for some type of communications audit activity is large and this will be reflected in the approaches taken in the book (although, broadly speaking, a problem-solving approach is assumed to be most applicable). The framework adopted will seek to provide guidance for tackling anything from a well-defined specific communications problem to the broader 'messy' problem that tends to involve the future of the company and in which communications may play only a small part.

In order to address the problems mentioned above, the subsequent chapter topics are as follows:

2   Background to communications auditing, or Why do a communications audit?
3   Techniques of communications auditing: DIY communications auditing
4   Communications equipment
5   Information and expertise
6   Complex communications problems: a systems approach

So far as possible each chapter has been designed to stand alone, so that readers can, if they wish, limit their attention to the parts most relevant to their particular interest.

Chapter 2 deals briefly with the need for communications auditing in organizations and discusses the benefits and costs. Chapter 3 describes the specific techniques available to audit communications, concentrating mainly on those techniques which might be applied without outside assistance, rather than those which may call for the use of external consultants. Chapter 4 is concerned with equipment that may be of interest to organizations currently seeking to improve their communications efficiency in order to solve specific problems. Chapter 5 gives guidance on how to obtain cost-effective advice in this area, in terms both of the available literature and of commercial consultancies. Chapter 6 offers the manager a framework for dealing with wider-ranging communication problems. The system methodologies described can also be usefully employed in other problem areas within the organization. (For example, they are a useful tool in seeking to understand and resolve interdepartmental conflict.) The methodologies are illustrated using one typical company situation and one case study based within a service organization.

This book has been written as a result of a research project into the current state of communications auditing in the UK. The project showed that there is an increasing use of communications audits by larger organizations, and a lack of awareness of the value of a communications audit by small to medium-sized firms. This book is aimed at helping to correct this lack of awareness and is therefore primarily oriented towards smaller and medium-sized firms. Managers in large corporations may also find it of value, since, especially in decentralized organizations, extra efficiency in communication is needed to keep sub-units working in concert. Certainly, most of the problems addressed may affect any size of organization.

To illustrate some of these problems, and increase awareness of the impact of poor communications, occasional examples will be provided in the text. The first of these follows:

In a large Midlands company, which carries out research on a commercial basis as one of its activities, a major new project had just been negotiated. In order to achieve the maximum input of ideas to carry out this task, a senior member of staff circulated relevant employees with an invitation to a seminar to discuss how the project could be most effectively handled. A few days later the same employees received a follow-up letter (from another senior member of staff) apologizing for the fact that the venue of the seminar had been omitted from the original invitation. Shortly after that, a third letter arrived which provided the same information as the first two letters, but this time came from the head of the company.

The fact that this was not an isolated failure was illustrated to the communications auditor by the next invitation sent out for a similar seminar. On this occasion the time and place were both specified and only one letter was sent out on the topic. Unfortunately, a sentence describing the background to the project was missing. Readers of the letter did not have to infer that something was missing from the letter; the blank space in the middle of a paragraph made it obvious!

At this point it became clear that a thorough audit of the systems of communications within the company was called for.

This simple example gives some indication of how organizations can waste resources of time and money by the inefficient use of communications. In this case, the losses were relatively small and consisted of:

(a) (i) Time losses of the senior members of the company in preparing unnecessary memos that largely duplicated information already sent out.
(ii) Time losses of the larger number of individuals who were in receipt of the memos in having to read unnecessary extra communications.

(b) Extra postage costs, both internal and external, associated with these extra communications.

(c) Less quantifiable costs in terms of loss of motivation/morale by staff presented with this evidence of managerial inefficiency and lack of cooperation on what should have been a simple communication task.

Senior management faced with this type of problem has to ask itself: How much is this a symptom of overall poor communications capability within the company?

2 Why communications auditing?

Management in organizations may be described as consisting of four main activities:

- Communication
- Control
- Coordination
- Planning.

It is only by the successful application of all these activities that an organization or group may meet its objectives. For reasons discussed earlier, now may be the time for the reader to audit the communications in his or her organization. This does not imply that checks are not also needed upon the systems of control, coordination and planning. However, it may be argued that good communications are vital to the carrying out of these three central activities, and, because of changes in communications technology, this field should be examined first. Further, an examination of any of the named activities will, in the real world, lead to some study of the others, as is apparent in typical projects carried out by consultancies specializing in communications auditing.

Before going any further, it is appropriate to provide some type of working definition of the term 'communications audit', for there is no overall consistency in the limited literature on this topic. Different authors use the term to cover a number of different meanings, some very limited and some too wide-ranging. For the purposes of this book, the communications audit will be defined as:

> 'The process whereby the communications within an organization are analysed by an internal or external consultant, with a view to increasing organizational efficiency.'

This meaning is primarily concerned with communication within the organization and so does not include any measurement of the organization's advertising or PR capability. However, some interactions with the environment do need to be included, for example, the systems used to communicate with clients/customers, or the ordering system used when purchasing from raw material suppliers. The accent will be upon systems of communication, rather than the measurement of the individual manager's capacity to communicate. It will not be assumed, as by some US authors, that the reader's organization has a communications department. Such departments are not common in small to medium-sized companies in the UK.

Why do a communications audit?

Goldhaber and Rogers (1979) illustrate the need for the use of the International Communication Association's communication audit by using two analogies. They note that companies need financial audits and individuals need physical check-ups. Both these types of check-up provide clients with information necessary to retain the 'health' of the system, be it individual or organizational. In the same way, communications audits provide an organization with advance information which may prevent serious breakdowns affecting overall performance. The objectives of the ICA communications audit may be rather broader than most small/medium UK organizations would require; but they are an interesting indication of the wider potential of this type of activity:

1 Determine the amount of the information underload or overload associated with the major *topics, sources and channels* of communication.
2 Evaluate the *quality of information* communicated from and/or to these sources.

3   Assess the *quality of communication relationships*, specifically measuring the extent of interpersonal trust, supportiveness, sociability and overall job satisfaction.

4   Identify the *operational communications networks* (for rumours, social and job-related messages), comparing them with planned or formal networks (prescribed by organizational charts).

5   Determine potential *bottlenecks and gatekeepers of information* by comparing actual communication roles of key personnel (isolates, liaisons, group members, etc.) with expected roles (provided by job descriptions, etc.).

6   Identify categories and examples of commonly occurring positive and negative *communication experiences and incidents*.

7   Describe individual, group and organizational patterns of *actual communication behaviours* related to sources, channels, topics, length and quality of interactions.

8   Provide general recommendations, derived from the Audit, which call for changes or improvements in attitudes, behaviours, practices and skills.

Emanuel (1985), also in the USA, provides some specific examples of why, and when, a communications audit should be carried out:

Some Reasons Why:

● To find out how well communications programs are working

● To diagnose current or potential communications problems or missed opportunities

● To evaluate a new communications policy or practice

● To assess the relationship of communications to other organizational operations on corporate and local levels

● To develop communications budgets

● To develop benchmarks

● To measure progress against previously established benchmarks

● To develop or restructure the communications function within an organization

● To provide background for developing formal communications policies and plans.

Some Times When:

● Major reorganization
● Merger or Acquisition
● New Management team
● Business Turndown
● External events cause concern
● Upcoming union negotiations.

Looking at the British literature on this topic, the present author's study, *Communications Audits: A UK Survey* (1986), found the following typical reasons for carrying out such audits, according to consultants working in this area:

(a)   *Prior* to a large-scale company restructuring or to a rationalization exercise.
(b)   *After* a large-scale company restructuring or rationalization exercise.
(c)   When there is a need to increase the motivation of employees.
(d)   When telephone bills are increasing rapidly, or are perceived to be too high.
(e)   When customers have difficulty making contact with the sales department.
(f)   When long-term plans and strategies are being developed.
(g)   When there is a need to check that managers and their subordinates see things in the same light (e.g. when a strike is threatened that will, with hindsight, be blamed upon poor management/union communications).
(h)   Before any decision is taken on the purchase of telecommunications hardware (eg. a new PABX).
(i)   When there are too many memos and not enough relevant information.
(j)   When labour turnover is too high.
(k)   When there is an *obvious* communications problem.
(l)   When a routine check of organizational effectiveness is required.

It may be useful to see the need for communications audits as occurring anywhere along a 'problem–planning' dimension. At one end, communications audits can be used to investigate and suggest solutions to specific problems. At the other end, when planning is required, communications audits produce a useful 'snapshot' of where the organization is now. Where you are now

Date	Time	Country	Area.City.Town	Dialled Number	Duration Mins Secs	Charge Band Rate	Units	Cost	
17/12/84	14.15.39	UK	LOCAL	9723423	2.08	L STD	2	£0.09	E
18/12/84	10.01.39	UK	LOCAL	2533548	3.00	L PEAK	2	£0.09	E
18/12/84	10.27.31	UK	OPERATOR	100	0.36	OP			E
18/12/84	14.15.39	UK	LOCAL	9723423	2.08	L STD	2	£0.09	E
18/12/84	14.28.43	UK	BURY ST EDMUNDS	0284463131	1.28	B STD	5	£0.24	E
19/12/84	9.39.39	UK	LOCAL	5009197	1.06	L PEAK	1	£0.05	E
19/12/84	12.22.39	UK	LOCAL	3607775	9.26	L PEAK	7	£0.33	E
19/12/84	14.04.39	UK	LOCAL	9723423	1.34	L STD	1	£0.05	E
19/12/84	14.13.31	UK	OPERATOR	100	8.08	OP			E
20/12/84	9.22.43	UK	ABERDEEN	0224229999	0.36	B1 PEAK	2	£0.09	E
20/12/84	10.11.39	UK	LOCAL	3635353	0.32	L PEAK	1	£0.05	E
20/12/84	13.34.39	UK	LOCAL	3607775	10.41	L STD	6	£0.28	E
20/12/84	14.06.39	UK	LOCAL	9723423	2.46	L STD	2	£0.24	E
21/12/84	10.53.39	UK	LOCAL	2533548	6.26	L PEAK	5	£0.24	E
21/12/84	14.04.39	UK	LOCAL	9723423	3.19	L STD	2	£0.09	E

**** UK LOCAL ****

	PEAK	STD	CHEAP
CALLS	16	25	0
AV. TIME	4.31	3.58	0.00
UNITS	56	62	0
COST	£2.46	£2.91	£0.00

** UK LONG DIST **

	PEAK	STD	CHEAP
CALLS	4	1	0
AV. TIME	2.44	1.28	0.00
UNITS	40	5	0
COST	£1.88	£0.24	£0.00

** INTERNATIONAL **

	PEAK	STD	CHEAP
CALLS	0	0	0
AV. TIME	0.00	0.00	0.00
UNITS	0	0	0
COST	£0.00	£0.00	£0.00

****** TOTAL ******

	PEAK	STD	CHEAP
CALLS	20	26	0
AV. TIME	4.10	3.52	0.00
UNITS	96	67	0
COST	£4.52	£3.15	£0.00

	TOT CALLS	TOTAL TIME	AV. TIME	UNITS	LOCAL	LONG DIST	INTERNAT.	TOTAL
OP	3	12.03	4.01					
EXTN	49	195.48	4.00	163	£5.55	£2.12	£0.00	£7.67
TOTAL	49	195.48	4.00	163	£5.55	£2.12	£0.00	£7.67

Figure 2.1 Printout from a telephone call logging device

is a valuable piece of information when planning how to get where you want to be in 6 months or 10 years. In this context, communications audits can provide a good benchmark.

How much is it going to cost?

The cost of a communications audit in terms of money and time depends on the size of the problem being tackled. In the example given at the end of the last chapter, the initial 'audit' could be seen as having taken place when a senior member of staff recognized the problem, and confirmed that it was not just a 'one-off' breakdown in communications. Subsequent actions to prevent the recurrence of the event could be a clarification of responsibilities for sending out the invitations between the three members of management involved, and the development of a checklist for preparation of such invitations in future. The time costs of such remedial action would be low. It would be necessary also to use some judgement as to whether this systems breakdown was a symptom of wider failures within the company. If this was the case, a more wide-ranging and thorough audit might be called for.

Another relatively low-cost and specific auditing exercise might involve the purchase of a simple telephone call logging device. Such devices are becoming increasingly popular because their continuous monitoring of the telephone system proves to be an effective method of controlling telecommunications costs. They are also useful in terms of budgeting control and costing allocations, such as the distribution of overheads (if telephone costs are considered as overheads). An example of a printout from a call logger installed in one of Britain's medium-sized manufacturing firms is shown in Figure 2.1.

A third, relatively specific, auditing exercise that has wide application is the evaluation of the organization's written communications by the Gunning 'Fog Index'. Robert Gunning developed his Fog Index as a measure of 'readability' for written messages, and it measures the approximate number of years of education a reader will have needed in order to understand a particular message. Indications are that most readers prefer to read well below their education levels. Popular magazines in the USA, for example, have a Fog Index of 5 or 6, while the *Wall Street Journal* has a Fog Index of around 11; studies of readers with a

PhD suggested that they are unwilling to spend prolonged periods reading material with a Fog Index above 13. However, according to one writer on business communication, business correspondence frequently reaches a Fog Index of 17 to 20.

The Fog Index can be calculated readily by taking a typical passage from a letter or report, for example, measuring such variables as length of sentences and number of syllables in the words used, and applying a simple mathematical formula. This method can be used by individual writers of reports, letters, memos to measure their communications ability. It can similarly be used to evaluate company handbooks and advertising/sales literature. If the Fog Index is too high for the intended reader, or audience, the chances of the message getting through effectively are reduced. Thus an appropriate Fog Index is required to maximize efficiency in written communication, whether the message is meant to motivate staff or pass on functional information. The details for the method of calculating the Fog Index are given in the next chapter.

At the other extreme, communications audits can cost tens of thousands of pounds, if the project they are associated with is large enough. For example, in the 1960s and 1970s large communications audit exercises were carried out as part of the 'Hardman' studies which looked at the possibilities for moving some civil servants' jobs from London to cheaper sites in the provinces. Extensive audits of communication activities of different government departments showed which ones could most easily be moved to places such as Swindon without damage to their functioning. Factors examined included an analysis of the need to attend face-to-face meetings and travel costs associated with communication activities.

Large companies also spend substantial sums upon communications audit activities which are aimed at ensuring that the company's communications policy is as effective as possible in motivating employees to work hard towards the fulfilment of organizational goals. In the case of organizations in the *Times Top 1000* with multi-site operations, the cost of surveying a relatively small number of employees (in percentage terms of the total workforce) in order to obtain a representative sample can be high. In the case of smaller companies, the absolute cost of such an exercise would be much lower, although its proportional cost in terms of employees' time is not likely to be less.

Associated with the cost factor is the issue of whether to use an external consultant, or internal personnel. The internal consultant could be the manager, or it might be staff in the personnel or management services departments (if the company has them). There are certain types of project (or circumstances) that tend to require the use of an external specialist consultant. For example, if the communications audit is to be a large one then it is worth seriously considering the use of external consultants, simply because internal staff are not likely to have the time both to carry out the audit and do their own jobs. Similarly, if specialist knowledge is called for in the purchase of computing or telecommunications equipment, the cost of a consultant's fee may well be justified. It may seem cheaper initially not to buy such technical advice, but, in view of the rapid changes occurring in telecommunications hardware, the old adage 'A little learning is a dangerous thing' is singularly appropriate. The advice of sales staff of telecoms manufacturers is potentially partisan, and technical journals offering advice frequently assume a level of background knowledge that not all managers have, however up to date they consider themselves.

On the other hand, motivation-oriented audits often only require the use of relatively simple and well-known techniques, such as questionnaires or structured interviews (which will be described later in this book). These may be more easily used by the manager, or the organization may already employ staff who have experience of questionnaire design, for example. Some communications problems can be solved simply by allocating oneself a period of time to stand back, define the problem, measure it in some way, and then develop a set of alternative solutions. The author has frequently had experiences in managing in an industrial situation where a particular problem was easily and permanently solved when time was taken out from the common 'crisis' management of day-to-day problems.

One further variable should be considered in deciding whether to bring in outside consultants – namely, the objectivity of the consultant. If an audit is carried out in a 'politically' sensitive organizational communications area by an internal member of staff, then that member of staff is open to accusations of bias. Bringing in an outside consultant reduces the danger of this charge, and therefore increases the chances of (radical) changes, which are recommended following the audit, being accepted by all groups in the organization.

Finally, in looking at costs, the problem of raising false

expectations needs to be considered. For example, if employees know that a communications audit is being carried out to improve communications between management and themselves, they might well respond positively and expectations could be raised about improvements in organizational practices in this area. If, after the audit, no changes occur, either due to lack of management commitment, or because the findings are embarrassing to particular senior managers, staff are likely to be demotivated. Thus there has to be a commitment to change at the top, and the manager concerned needs to have the authority to push through any changes indicated by the audit.

Conclusions

Communications audits involve costs in terms of time and money for the organization. If they are carried out well, and followed through, the benefits of fewer problems, greater efficiency and higher motivation of employees will usually justify the costs, and, indeed, produce a net profit for the organization concerned.

3 The techniques of communications auditing

Interviews with a number of leading communications-oriented consultancies suggested that the following eight techniques are the most widely used in auditing communications in the UK. In order of descending frequency of usage they are:

- Structured interviews
- Unstructured interviews
- Questionnaires
- Group discussions
- Network analysis or socio-grams
- Communications diaries
- Telephone call logging/monitoring
- In tray/out tray analysis

Other techniques used by consultants include:

- Checking and analysing telephone bills.
- Looking at the house newspaper, videos and training films, etc.
- Reviewing all printed matter.
- Carrying out a structured systems analysis.
- Drawing a picture of the principal information flows.
- Running computer simulation models of proposed networks to evaluate traffic flow, etc.
- Use of the Delphi forecasting technique.
- Monitoring telex usage.
- Mail tagging.

The choice of technique is very much dependent upon the objectives of the audit and some techniques are applicable in many cases, whilst others are specifically oriented to individual aspects of the communications process. In order to aid selection of the most relevant techniques, each description will be prefaced by examples of circumstances in which the technique might most usefully be used. The most widely applicable methods from the above listings will be described first. Other techniques not mentioned above will be described when they are likely to be of particular use to the manager in the small to medium-sized organization. The amount of detail given for a particular technique will vary according to the author's assessment of the likelihood of its usefulness for personal applications by the reader. Hence information will be given in some detail on how to design questionnaires, as this is something that individual managers can do themselves cost-effectively. The preparation of computer simulation models of traffic flows, in contrast, will not be described. Such problems will almost always require outside assistance.

Problem definition

Usage

Although problem definition was not mentioned explicitly by communications consultants, it is a necessary component of any problem-solving approach.

Problem identification/description/definition may be relatively simple and speedy or it may be complex and lengthy. It may be the initial step that leads into many other activities that produce a solution, or it may be the big step that produces a solution in itself. In this section we shall be concentrating upon problems that are relatively easy to define, describe, or identify. An approach to the more complex organizational problems that have a communications audit component is described in Chapter 6.

Generally a problem may be seen as something that produces a tension or stress within a system, person or organization. When the problem is solved the tension is released or removed. In this context the tension may be the subjective feeling by a senior manager that his subordinates are not working as hard as they could, due to a lack of commitment to organizational goals. Alternatively, it may be the more specific tension associated, for example, with the fact that every time the manager wishes to telephone a customer, there is a substantial delay in getting a response from the company switchboard before the call can be made.

At this stage it is only necessary to ask four questions, answer them, and then act accordingly. These are:

1 Is there a (communications-related) problem?
2 What is the problem? (It is useful to write out at this stage one sentence which starts with 'The problem is ...'.)
3 Is some (further) expenditure of time and/or money justified in attempting to achieve a solution?
4 Given the preliminary statement of the problem, what techniques are called for to investigate it further?

If the answer to question 1 is 'No', then this book may be returned to the shelf for the time being. If the answer is 'Yes', then questions 2 and 3 should be answered after some *limited* thought. (Refinement or complete thoroughness is not called for at this stage of problem solving.) When this has been done, it will be possible to answer the fourth question by referring to the preface sections of each of the techniques described in this chapter.

Having carried out this activity it is possible to commence the communications audit, but that does not mean the above four questions are finished with. Instead they should be repeated regularly throughout the audit as further information is gathered. Hence, with increased knowledge the problem becomes redefined or a negative answer to question 3 determines that further effort is not worthwhile, and the process should be stopped. Thus the problem definition technique in this context is an iterative one.

The interview

Interviews may be described as conversations with specified purposes. In the context of communications auditing they may be divided into two types: the unstructured interview or the structured interview, although in a practical situation it is possible for an interview to contain a structured section and an unstructured section. Designing a structured interview has common elements with the designing of a questionnaire, in that with both these techniques the person providing the information is asked to provide specific and relatively 'closed' answers to all the appropriate questions decided upon in advance. In the case of an unstructured interview the responses of the information-provider are instrumental in determining questions that follow, i.e. the exchange is interactive in that feedback in the form of answers influences the choice of later questions.

In both the structured and unstructured interview a number of key items need to be considered:

(a) Objective of interview.
(b) Setting for interview.
(c) Length of interview.
(d) Interview skills.
(e) Preparation for interview.
(f) Recording of interview.

Objective of interview

In the context of this book objectives are likely to be concerned with gaining information related to particular communications problems/issues. The objective of the interview will be to some extent determined by the problem definition stage mentioned earlier, and thus there are many potential specific objectives. There is little purpose in trying to give advice on the setting of particular objectives, because of the potential variety involved. The main point is that the interviewer should know his/her own objective(s) before the interview starts, on the grounds that if you know where you are going, it is normally easier to get there!

Setting for interview

The interview has to be carried out somewhere, and the choice of venue requires some thought in view of its potential impact on the quality and quantity of information being received. On some occasions casually wandering into someone's office and asking for a few minutes of their time might be sufficient, and even psychologically appropriate. On other occasions it may be necessary to arrange the interview in advance and hold it in a conference room away from the normal interruptions of telephones and colleagues.

If a manager is interviewing a subordinate about methods of improving internal paper work systems, for example, creativity may not be enhanced if the manager places the barrier of his/her desk between them, with all its implications of manager–subordinate roles. A neutral setting with discussion over a cup of coffee is more likely to create an atmosphere conducive to idea generation.

Length of interview

In the same way that it is worthwhile identifying an objective, it is of value to set a target for how long the interview should last. Besides giving the interviewee some idea of how long he or she will need to allocate in planning their day, it encourages concentration and efficiency in both parties.

Interview skills

Most of the skills of interviewing relate to the communication process and are concerned with ensuring that the right information passes in both directions. Thus interviewers have to ensure that what they say does not bias the response of the person being interviewed. Also questions have to be asked in such a way as to encourage the interviewee to speak at appropriate length. The choice of the type of question is important in both these cases:

- *Open questions* encourage interviewees to speak at some length and elicit feelings and attitudes as well as facts. For example, 'What do you think of the communications in this department?'
- *Closed questions* are intended to elicit short one-word answers, namely Yes or No. For example, 'Do you have access to an external telephone?'
- *Specific questions* similarly are aimed at provoking a specific factual answer. For example, 'How many times per day do you use your computer terminal for external communications?'
- *Reflective questions* are a response to an answer given by the interviewee that encourages further comment. These encour-

age the person to deal with the topic in more depth. For example, if the interviewee says that her supervisor doesn't give her enough information to make planning decisions, the question 'What type of planning decisions?' is likely to elicit further details on the meaning of the term 'planning decisions' for the interviewee.

- *Leading questions* are useful if you have made up your mind on the topic and wish to encourage agreement rather than honest opinions! An example of this is the statement 'I think communications in this company are excellent, don't you?'
- *Hypothetical questions* are useful in encouraging interviewers to think ahead. For example, 'If money was no object, how would you improve communications with our salesforce when they are out selling?'

Having chosen the most relevant questions and framed them appropriately, skill is required in asking them and in listening to the answers. The fundamental problem is to break down, as far as possible, the barriers to frank discussion. (These are most apparent when interviewees are being asked questions that require the expression of opinions or attitudes rather than the simple statement of facts.) There is substantial literature on this topic, but probably the most important point for the manager interviewing colleagues of various levels is that interviewees need to be put at ease, and then, when they are talking, given verbal and non-verbal cues that encourage them to continue (if what they are saying is considered relevant). Besides using reflective questions, as mentioned above, the interviewer needs to look interested and interject the occasional 'mmm', 'uh-huh' or 'that's interesting'. It is also useful to summarize what the interviewee has said periodically to confirm that their points have been understood.

Preparation for interview

Some interviews require no detailed preparation other than setting objectives and a time and place. Frequently, however, it is necessary to marshal some facts before starting. For example, the interviewer may find it useful to have read through the personal file of the individual being interviewed. Alternatively some background reading/information search may be necessary to give information on matters of fact that the interview is likely to raise. Also it is possible, if the interview is one of a series, that the interviewer may need to refresh his/her memory on decisions taken subsequent to the last interview.

Recording of interview

Some record of the interview is normally necessary. The biggest problems associated with recording what has been said relate to the effects upon the interviewee of the recording process, and the use to which the record is to be put.

Some interviewers who are seeking to discuss topics that seem threatening to the interviewee, or confidential in nature, rely on memory and writing up the interview after it has taken place. In some circumstances the sight of a tape recorder or notepad can cause the interviewee to clam up completely.

If a complete record is needed, a tape recording is the best method. A transcript may then be typed up later, or the tape may be referred to directly. It should be noted, however, that the physical handling and searching of tapes for particular items is not easy. This method is most useful as an insurance policy, as illustrated in the Watergate affair.

The most common method of recording is for the interviewer to take notes during the interview. This method is visible and interferes to some extent with the interviewer's ability to listen to what is being said. However, it does show the interviewee that what is being said is important enough to be written down, and hence has a potential advantage. One variation on this method that the author has found valuable is the writing down of only a few key words associated with the interviewee's answers. These act as a memory aid for the preparation of a more complete transcript after the interview, and cut down the amount of recording activity in the interview itself. Another variation is to have a third person present just to record what is being said; but in most circumstances this is likely to reduce the participant's willingness to speak freely as it increases the formality of the situation.

The unstructured interview

Usage

This technique may be seen as a development of the problem definition in that it incorporates the views of others into the definition process. It is a very common technique in the problem-solving process. It may usefully be applied:

(a) When the manager wishes to clarify or develop his or her thoughts on the issue or problem.
(b) When the problem concerns broader issues, such as planning communications policy for the next five/ten years.
(c) When there are obvious differences of perception of the problems by different personnel within the company.
(d) When the manager concerned wishes to 'prime' other members of the organization prior to substantial organizational change.

In this technique we may include the extremes from the casual informal discussion between colleagues to the practised interventions of communications consultants brought in to look at the particular area in depth.

The end product of the unstructured interview

Typically at the beginning of an unstructured interview one has a small number of topics around which discussion can be based. These topics will primarily be developed by open, hypothetical and reflective questions. At the end of the interview the information gained has to be processed in a way that is functional to the solution of the perceived problem. How this is done will be determined by the particular problem, but it is worthwhile reconsidering the questions from the problem definition stage at this point. Specifically the problem definition will now be a different statement or set of statements, as a consequence of the extra knowledge gained through the interview(s).

The structured interview

Usage

The structured interview is a useful tool when the investigator is aware of all the variables to be studied and is primarily concerned with collecting empirical evidence about these variables within an organization. Hence, if you are seeking to discover whether sales reports from representatives are being received by everyone who needs them in the company, and by no one who does not, a structured interview is appropriate. Variables to be measured in this case might be: (a) who receives the reports, (b) who does not receive them, (c) what they are used for by the recipients, (d) how highly they are valued as an information source. Structured interviews are the most common technique used by consultants who carry out communications audits, as experience often enables them to predict the most likely critical variables in many communication system evaluations.

The process of designing a structured interview is very similar to that of designing a self-completion questionnaire. The structured interview has the advantage that the interviewee can ask for clarification of any questions not understood. Its main disadvantage when compared with the self-completion questionnaire is the increased costs, especially in terms of the interviewer's time. In the specific context of communications auditing available evidence suggest that structured interviews are used when relatively small numbers of people are being sampled and self completion questionnaires are used when large organizational populations are being sampled. Descriptions of the two techniques that follow are based upon this assumption.

The interview schedule has to be devised so that it suits the audit's objectives and is appropriate to the nature of the interviewees. The questions need to be clear and unambiguous so that potential errors by interviewees are minimized. Care needs to be taken in ensuring that all important variables are included. The schedule and each individual question should be designed in a way that maximizes the chances of interviewees being interested in the

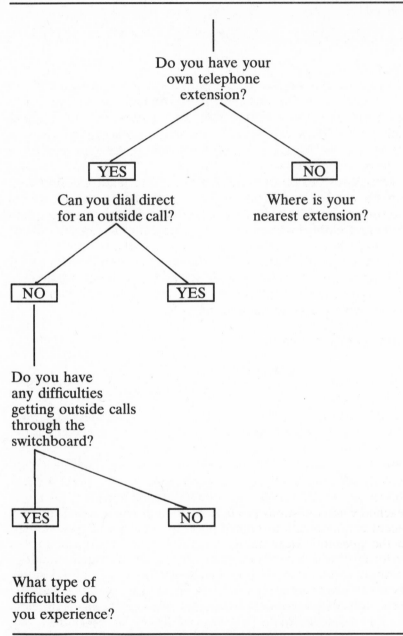

Figure 3.1   Flowchart for an audit on telephone usage

topic. Questions need to be phrased so that honesty in replies is encouraged, and bias of interviewers is reduced to a minimum.

Design of interview schedule

The designer must move from a general framework of information needs (i.e. the important variables relating to the particular audit) to an organized set of questions. Flow charts are useful in carrying out this process especially when the answer to one question determines whether or not the next two questions (for example) are applicable. Figure 3.1 represents a flow chart for part of an audit on telephone usage.

Once this type of framework is outlined the detailed design work can be carried out. This includes formulating the individual questions, putting the questions and sections in an appropriate order and adding instructions and signposts for the interviewer. At this stage some thought should be given to the length of the interview. Interest in the topic will vary between individuals, as will the length of their attention span. Forty minutes may be a useful guideline for interviews in terms of the time that most people will be able to maintain interest.

Formulating questions

Apart from the basic problem of ensuring that the interviewee can understand the questions there are other potential problems in asking questions. Some of these apply to all questions whilst others occur with only a minority of the questions that might be included in a communications audit.

Problems of memory Most questions in communications audit interviews do not stretch into the past to any great extent. However, the limitations of a person's memory can be easily reached when questions relate to routine or trivial details of even recent communications behaviour. The accuracy of the response to the question 'How many times did your boss speak to you yesterday?' will depend, for example, on the average amount of communication between boss and subordinate. If your boss only speaks to you twice a week it is easy to answer the above question accurately. If levels of everyday communications are high, as in the case of a managing director and his or her secretary, then it becomes more difficult to recall the episodes clearly and hence quantify them. In contrast, the critical incident technique described later in this chapter is less sensitive to memory losses. Another standard technique (also described later in this chapter) is the communications diary in which the person concerned records all his/her communication events as they occur.

Questions that make excessive demands upon memory are also likely to provide inaccurate data because individuals generally tend to provide a 'guesstimate' rather than admit that they can't remember.

Difficult or sensitive questions The problem of sensitive questions most commonly arises when research is being done in areas related to sexual or criminal behaviour. Those topics do not normally arise in communications auditing, but within organizations there are potential taboo subjects that are not openly discussed. Such subjects might be the incompetence of a particular manager or member of staff. Alternatively, suppose that the company has just spent £20000 on a data communications system only to find that it does not really conform to its requirements and there is another, better, system available for £10000. Everyone may be aware of this problem, but it might not be politically acceptable to admit the mistake. Linked to this problem is the difficulty of getting accurate answers when an honest reply will amount to a confession that the interviewee is not conforming with company policy. If there is a standing order that all non-urgent telephone calls should be made after 1.00 pm the answers to the question 'How many telephone calls did you make between 9.00 am and 1.00 pm?' might be censored at least.

In some circumstances it is not possible to ask such questions sensibly in a formal interview; other sources such as the grapevine may have to be used. Sometimes, however, the phrasing of the question can be designed to maximize the chances of honest reply. For example, a company may have introduced a team briefing scheme and one year later wants to check whether its different divisions are still carrying out the briefings regularly. The two forms of the question below may be expected to obtain differing degrees of honesty in reply.

Q1 Have you been holding team briefings every week in this department as specified in company policy?

Q2 Some departments appear to find little demand for team briefings and have only been holding them periodically. Have you also found a similar lack of interest and amended the frequency of your briefings as well?

Sensitive questions in organizations are commonly those that imply a 'right' or 'wrong' answer that has implications for the person's career. In such circumstances it is necessary to stress confidentiality, assuring the interviewee that any remarks made by him or her will not be attributed to them without permission. When the interviewer is also the interviewee's line manager then the working relationship, more than anything, will determine the willingness or otherwise of the subordinate to answer sensitive questions.

Finally, a technique that may be of value when addressing sensitive issues is the use of the provocative question. For example, 'Don't you think that senior management pass on planning information to middle management so incompetently that they all ought to be asked to resign?' Besides asking a question that raises a specific issue about downward communication in the organization, this question alerts the interviewee to the fact that topics of conversation that are normally taboo might be open to debate in the interview.

Zoning in A frequent mistake in interviewing is to assume a level of knowledge by an interviewee that does not exist. It is thus important at the beginning of the interview to establish that there is some common knowledge on the topic under inspection. For example, you may have a detailed knowledge of a particular system of communications within the organization that means you are the company expert on it. Questions to others about the system that assume a similar level of knowledge will promote blank looks or attempts to give the impression of knowledge that does not exist. Therefore, before asking your colleagues which particular PABX they think you should buy to replace the present manual internal telephone exchange, check to see if they know what PABX means.

Other considerations are also important when asking the first few questions of an interview, in that the right type of question appropriately asked helps the whole interview get off to a good start. Initial questions, besides setting the scene and checking common levels of knowledge, should therefore be easy to answer and not sensitive. It may even be worth asking questions whose answers you don't need to know so that the interviewee can obtain the satisfaction of giving some straightforward and apparently relevant information. Difficult or sensitive questions should be saved for the middle of the interview, and should also be followed by some more neutral questions, so that the interviewee does not

29

finish the interview feeling uneasy or threatened. It is also important to thank all interviewees for their time regardless of their rank within the organization.

Clarity and understanding Your questions obviously need to be understood by the interviewee and should be unambiguous. The simplest way to test this is by doing a pilot interview on someone similar to those to be interviewed. It is necessary to explain to this person that you are more interested in getting feedback on the questions than in his/her particular answers.

The end product of the structured interview

At the end of a structured interview exercise there are two broad options:

(a)   If the variables that were identified prior to the design of the interview appear to have been appropriate and complete, it may be possible to decide upon the evidence available how the particular communications issue is to be dealt with. Referring back to the earlier example of reports on visits by sales representatives, a typical outcome could be the decisions: (i) to circulate extra copies of the reports to R&D staff to help them in the development of new products; (ii) to stop sending copies to the production department, who do not actually read them; (iii) to ask representatives to include in each report information on whether the volume of business with the particular customer is falling, rising or remaining approximately level.

(b)   The interviews may show a need for more information before recommendations can be made. Typically this might lead to extending the interview schedule or sample. Alternatively a self-completion questionnaire to be more widely circulated may be called for.

The same general comments apply to questionnaire design as to the design of an interview schedule, but there is one critical difference relating to matters of understanding. It is not possible for the information provider to ask for clarification of an ambiguous question. For this reason extra care is required in designing questions and in piloting the questionnaire. Also, as an interviewer is not there to motivate the individual to provide the information required, there is a greater danger of non-completion.

Design factors for this technique may be considered under the following headings:

(a)   Introductory letter
(b)   Length of questionnaire
(c)   Confidentiality/anonymity
(d)   Layout
(e)   Bias in questions
(f)   Measuring attitudes
(g)   Response rates
(h)   Using questionnaire results.

Self-completion questionnaire

Usage

The self-completion questionnaire has several similarities to the structured interview and many of the comments made in relation to the structured interview apply. It may typically be used rather than a structured interview when we wish to eliminate, or reduce, the costs of interviewer time. Thus, if the sample is very large or it is important to get the information quickly, a self-completion questionnaire is appropriate. It is potentially more confidential than a structured interview. It is widely used by consultants seeking to investigate the effectiveness of communications in organizations, in the context of motivation of employees. Attitude measures may be incorporated so that questionnaires may be used to test the perceptions the workforce have of their organization, as well as dealing with specific issues. In the former case the same questionnaire could be used before and after a big organizational change in order to monitor its effects.

The introductory letter

A typical self-completion questionnaire in a communications audit may be handed to the person who is to fill it in, or he/she may receive it via the (internal) post. As with any of the techniques described so far, the respondent has to be motivated to provide the relevant information. The introductory letter or covering letter that goes with the questionnaire is often the first step in generating this motivation. As such it should be brief and to the point, politely requesting that the respondent give some of his/her time and effort to the questionnaire's completion. The purpose of the exercise should be explained in general terms, but not in such detail as to bias the response. General information should be provided regarding what is to be done with the data when received and what types of consequence might follow when the exercise has been completed. Feedback on the results is normally offered when sending out unsolicited self-completion questionnaires to the general public, as an inducement. This may be appropriate in this context as well.

Length of questionnaire

A really lengthy questionnaire may induce a potential respondent to consign it to the waste paper basket without further ado. Alternatively, questionnaires that exclude vital variables in order to be brief are a waste of time and effort. The decision on the actual length must be balanced according to these considerations. Other factors in this calculation include:

(a) The amount of organizational power that you have to induce completion of the questionnaire.
(b) The amount of time/effort available for processing the information received in completed questionnaires.
(c) The use of sneaky tricks, such as photo reduction, which makes the questionnaire appear shorter because it is physically less bulky.

Anonymity and confidentiality

Providing information in questionnaires may have consequences for the respondents: 'Honesty may damage your career prospects'. Because of this, it is necessary to spell out in the covering letter, or elsewhere, issues relating to the protection of sources. Some respondents may be happy for you to quote them by name. Others may be prepared to provide information only when they can see that the response cannot be identified as theirs, even by you as the communications auditor. Whatever the approach you decide upon, it is appropriate on both practical and moral grounds to give relevant details in any covering letter. Questionnaires that do not request the respondent's name are inconvenient in that you cannot take follow-up action, such as returning to the respondent to ask further questions. Also this approach prevents the efficient use of reminder letters to those who have not returned their question-naires after a suitable length of time. However, the potential insights into the functioning of the organization that complete anonymity can provide may not be available with any other procedure.

Layout of questionnaire

Motivating the respondent to start filling in the questionnaire is again a primary concern. Hence the layout should be such that the overall impression is one of simplicity. This means, in particular, that the questions should not be cramped and difficult to read. Understanding should be enhanced by the use of subsections for questions which relate to a similar topic. Also allowance has to be made for the estimated length of answer for each question so that the respondents have enough room to answer fully.

The use of simple, factual, non-threatening questions is advisable at the start of the questionnaire. More difficult questions (i.e. those that require more thought or commitment to the question-naire) should be saved until the respondent is committed to completion of the questionnaire because of the time he or she has already invested.

Consistency in design helps if it is possible. Don't switch from asking respondents to tick appropriate boxes to asking them to delete words unless it is really necessary. Finally, it may be obvious to you that respondents could tick more than one answer on a list of alternatives for a particular question; it does not fol-low that the respondent has your insight or knowledge. Therefore, give adequate instructions on how the question should/can be answered.

Bias in questions

There are many ways that a badly worded question can push a respon-dent in a particular direction not intended by the communications auditor. The following examples are three common types of bias.

Poor design	*Better design*
More and more people have experience of local area networks nowadays. Have you ever used one? 1 Yes 2 No	Have you ever used a local area network? 1 Yes 2 No
If you had to choose a new PABX would you choose (a) The IBM XYZ model (which is the most popular in sales terms now) (b) The GEC ABC model (which is the second most popular model)	If you had to choose a new PABX would you choose (a) The IBM XYZ model (b) The GEC ABC model
Do you think that morale in your department is (a) Excellent (b) Very good (c) Good (d) Acceptable (e) Average	Do you think that morale in your department is (a) Very good (b) Good (c) Average (d) Poor (e) Very poor

Measuring attitudes

Attitudes affect behaviour in organizations and so have to be assessed in some types of communications audits, especially those which are concerned with motivation of employees. Attitudes may be measured using various types of scale which allow the attitude to be quantified in some way. The Likert scale is one of the most common measures and can be presented in various forms; for example: 'Please indicate, by ticking the appropriate box, how much you agree or disagree with the following statement!

'I spend too much time filling in forms and report sheets in my job.'

Strongly agree ☐

Agree ☐

Neither agree nor disagree ☐

Disagree ☐

Strongly disagree ☐

[The alternatives may also be presented thus:

| Strongly Agree | Agree | Neither Agree nor disagree | Disagree | Strongly Disagree |

O————————O————————O————————O————————O

with the request to mark a point on the scale.]

Numerical values can then be associated with each point on such a scale as follows:

Strongly agree   = 5
Agree   = 4
Neutral   = 3
Disagree   = 2
Strongly disagree = 1

and average values for each question can be calculated for a group of individuals. In this way it is possible to calculate whether the attitudes of staff in two different departments differ significantly.

Response rates

Researchers sending out large numbers of unsolicited questionnaires are faced with the problem of ensuring that as large a proportion of recipients as possible reply. This is not likely to be such a problem with an internally conducted organizational questionnaire, as the sample being surveyed are more likely to be interested in the questions being asked. However, it is still possible that the proportion of people who do reply are not representative of the whole sample, and therefore any conclusions based upon their replies alone might be invalid. Thus a questionnaire sent to all members of a company to evaluate corporate morale may be answered in greater proportions by those who are very unhappy with things at present, and are taking the opportunity to complain through the questionnaire. The higher the response rate the less the likelihood of this type of inaccuracy occurring.

Variables that affect response rates are typically

(a) level of interest in topic by respondent;
(b) quality of introductory letter;
(c) inclusion of addressed envelope for response;
(d) reminder letters sent out to those who have not replied after a period of 1–2 weeks. Common practice is to send one reminder letter followed by a second if the first one is not effective;
(e) financial or other inducements.

Using questionnaire results

When the questionnaires have been completed and returned, it is necessary to reduce the mass of data they contain to useful information upon which decisions can be based. This is an activity that normally involves a substantial amount of 'number-crunching'. The number-crunching may be done manually with the aid of a calculator or more sensibly as the volume of data increases by the use of a computer package. One common technique is to provide a coding column down the right hand side of the questionnaire page for the insertion of numerical codes associated with each answer. In the following example a scale of 1 to 5 is used in classifying the answers to questions which measure attitudes or factual information related to the organizational climate.

Code

1 How satisfied are you that the training/induction the company gave you was sufficient and appropriate to your needs?

4

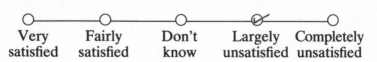

| Very satisfied | Fairly satisfied | Don't know | Largely unsatisfied | Completely unsatisfied |

2   How much freedom do you have to do your job in your own way?

2

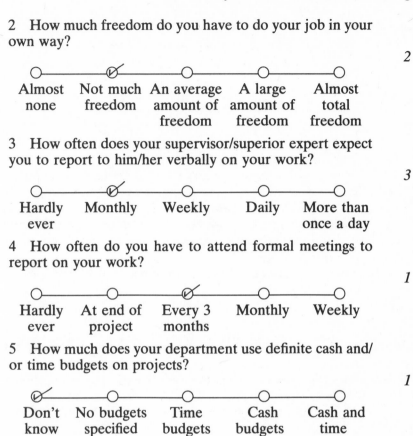

| Almost none | Not much freedom | An average amount of freedom | A large amount of freedom | Almost total freedom |

3   How often does your supervisor/superior expert expect you to report to him/her verbally on your work?

3

| Hardly ever | Monthly | Weekly | Daily | More than once a day |

4   How often do you have to attend formal meetings to report on your work?

1

| Hardly ever | At end of project | Every 3 months | Monthly | Weekly |

5   How much does your department use definite cash and/or time budgets on projects?

1

| Don't know | No budgets specified | Time budgets | Cash budgets | Cash and time budgets used |

Using the codes for each question it is then a relatively simple matter to seek correlations between job satisfaction and communication patterns, for example. Equally the data can be used to take averages for different departments and see how they compare with each other. Thus it is possible to attempt to relate varying levels of morale in different departments to differing communication practices.

To do this, statistical techniques are required to calculate correlations and to ensure that differences noted in the variables are statistically significant. It is not possible to discuss these techniques here, but there is no shortage of books on the topic. However, it is worth noting that when doing analysis on relatively small samples, i.e. less than 30, non-parametric statistical techniques are called for, rather than the more common parametric ones which assume 'normal' distributions in the samples being analysed.

Group discussions

Usage

Group discussions (or group interviews) can principally be used in two ways. They are both concerned with obtaining 'new' information or generating ideas. The former usage aims to obtain some measure of the attitudes and perceived problems associated with organizational communications from the point of view of groups working within the organization, for example, shopfloor workers, clerical officers, middle managers or R&D staff. The latter usage is oriented towards problem solving or forward planning, and the group interview is used to concentrate thought and stimulate ideas that may not arise when individuals are working separately on a particular problem.

Group discussions may be useful at various stages of the auditing process, depending on the particular topic at issue. Group discussions allow information to be gathered from a number of people at once and thus have advantages in terms of the auditor's time. They are a useful tool for providing general information about behaviour and attitudes and allow the auditor to see how people interact on a particular topic and, specifically, how they react to disagreement with their own viewpoint. Group discussions cannot, however, provide the detailed information about an individual's characteristics and background that may be obtained from individual interviews. They are similar to individual interviews in that the auditor must decide in advance to what degree they are to be structured.

Although some issues are difficult to handle in group discussion, it generally seems that people may admit to things in a group that they would not admit to in private. Embarrassment or reticence about topics not normally discussed openly is reduced when people can identify with others and hear them being open and frank. Thus in such situations individuals may feel brave enough to bring up issues that would be too threatening or challenging on a one-to-one basis. For example, issues such as their own competence as a communicator may be raised, if someone else sets an example by describing their own perceived shortcomings. Alternatively, problems caused by a more senior member of staff may come out in the open for the first time, if people in the group have the chance to discuss common experiences.

Managing a group discussion

The physical setting up of a group discussion is as important as for an individual interview and many of the comments made with regard to interviews apply here. There are, of course, other factors to consider, because more than two people are involved.

Group size: Too large a group means that some people do not get a chance to speak; too small a group may not have the 'critical mass' necessary to generate discussion and ideas. A common size of group is about seven or eight plus the auditor.

Getting everyone to speak: If the discussion is fairly structured then it is possible for the auditor to ask each person in turn for their views. This ensures everyone has a chance to speak but it can be a tedious method and does not encourage the free flow of conversation. The alternative is to let the group decide who will speak and in such circumstances a number of individuals normally dominate the conversation. In this format with eight people in the group, discussion can go on for over an hour with perhaps two or three group members never speaking at all. A compromise solution is to start by asking everyone to give their views on a particular topic and then leave things to the group. In this method all participants have been 'primed' and spoken once, and so the quieter, more introvert members are encouraged to continue to contribute.

A similar problem is that of the individual or individuals who dominate the conversation to the exclusion of all others. Frequently, this is most apparent at the beginning of discussion groups, and as time elapses the other group members assert themselves and control the flow of conversation. Occasionally this latter effect does not occur and then it is necessary for the auditor to use his or her social skills to dampen down the more voluble member, so that others get a chance to speak.

Mix of group: This is determined by the individual communications topics. Sometimes the group may be chosen to be very homogenous, e.g. a group of typists from within one department. At other times a spread of departments and tasks is called for, e.g. maintenance manager, private secretary, shopfloor worker, middle manager, R&D scientist, clerical officer. The former group might be called for when the system of typing/dispatching internal mail in the company is being rationalized. The latter group would be appropriate when seeking an evaluation of company needs.

Priming the group: In some circumstances it is advisable to give group members advance warning in some detail of the topic under discussion, so that they can do some preliminary thinking or fact finding. This is particularly appropriate in a problem-solving scenario. In other circumstances only the most general of advance indications is called for. This prevents people having discussed the topic so much informally, in advance, that they have nothing left to say at the proper group discussion.

Recording the discussion: The use of a tape recorder and microphone is still likely to inhibit conversation, at least initially, but less so than in a one-to-one interview. In view of the increased load on the auditor who is managing the group discussion (*vis-à-vis* a one-to-one interview) there is more reason to use a tape recorder.

Tea and biscuits: Serving tea and biscuits before the discussion helps people to relax.

Layout of the room: Chairs should be in a circle or semicircle so that all members of a group can see each other. It has been found that people sitting in corners (or too close to the discussion organizer) tend to get overlooked. This often causes them to resort to distracting subgroup discussions with their immediate neighbours.

In an American study a number of senior managers in several organizations were asked to select an immediate subordinate with whose work they were thoroughly familiar. They were then asked to define his role (including principal responsibilities, priorities amongst the responsibilities and qualifications required for the job). These subordinates were then requested to define their own roles independently with respect to the same variables. The level of agreement between members of the pairs was about 35 per cent.

The example above illustrates one important reason for a communications audit exercise; in this particular case a group discussion would be an appropriate technique to provide relevant information. This problem potentially exists with all organizations between any subordinate and his/her supervisor. Group discussions may be used to specify accurately perceived role discrepancies between particular types of supervisors and subordinates.

Thus, a sample of area sales managers might be chosen for a group discussion on the nature of their sales representatives' jobs. Then a similar group discussion is carried out with the sales representatives themselves dealing with their own jobs (and possibly those of their managers). The auditor can then pinpoint any serious discrepancies and make changes in communication practice if appropriate. He or she will also have been able to pick up any problems that both groups have at present and will simultaneously gain some measure of group morale. (The example of sales managers and representatives was chosen because typically sales managers are sales representatives who have been promoted. There is thus a tendency for them to assume they understand the job fully, and so be potentially cut off or ignore signals from their staff about task characteristics which may have changed since they were doing the job themselves.)

A communications consultancy was called in to look at communications problems being experienced by a very large British organization, and to make recommendations for its communications policies for the future. As part of this brief the consultants used group discussions in the following ways:

(a) With senior managers to identify the important communications systems within the organization, e.g. (i) movements of files, containing information about clients, within the organization, (ii) internal/

external telephone systems and (iii) flow of inter-departmental memoranda.

(b) With individual system users to help them identify particular problems in the system and to develop solutions.

(c) With senior managers to ask where they wanted the organization to be in five years so that communications policy could be developed within the context of organizational goals.

This technique and others enabled the consultants to recommend and help incorporate changes in the main internal communication systems. These changes removed problems and increased efficiency. In the longer term the group discussions encouraged the senior management to take a more positive posture to long-term planning, and to incorporate a knowledge of changing IT capabilities into their plans.

Network analysis

Usage

Techniques described so far have concerned obtaining information from individuals or groups. Network analysis is a technique that combines information provided by such techniques to give a 'map' of information flows within the organization or selected parts of it. It is therefore of value when an overall picture is called for, as might be required when considering company restructuring or major problem solving. It allows the auditor to identify both key communicators and those who communicate very little. It is one way of gaining an organizational overview of communication behaviours that can highlight present and potential problems.

Identifying and mapping communication networks

To identify a communications network it is necessary to obtain from individuals information on whom they communicate with and how frequently they do this. Often questions are also asked about the volume or importance of the communications. Doing this with appropriate groups within the organization enables 'maps' indicating communication routeways to be produced. The questions necessary to generate such 'maps' may be included in a more general communications-related questionnaire. Alternatively, an audit may include an element specifically designed to provide a recognizable network as the end-product. The example given below is the instrument used by the ICA (a US-based organization) when they carry out a network analysis as part of a communications audit.

NETWORK ANALYSIS (ICA INSTRUMENT)

As part of our study we would like you to complete this communication flow form. Although people's names are included here, your individual responses will not be made available to anyone in the organization. The purpose of this part of the audit is to assess quickly and efficiently the ability of the communication network to provide people with the information they need to do their jobs effectively and happily.

As you complete this form we want you to think about the people you usually communicate with in a typical work day. This includes face-to-face interaction, telephone calls, and written memos.

You will notice that we have asked about two different channels of communication. In the first, we want you to think of the times you communicate (sending and receiving) about work related matters through the formal organizational structure (e.g. committee or staff meetings, memos, official notices – oral or written – business communications).

In the second question, we want you to think of the times you communicate through the informal (grapevine) structure (e.g. chance conversations, spontaneous meetings, personal notes and phone calls).

To fill in the form, you should:

1   Find your name on the list and circle it.
2   Write the ID number found to the right of your name below.

3   Scan down the list of names until you locate a person with whom you usually communicate in a typical work day.
4   Decide whether each communication is part of either the formal or informal structure.
5   Write the number of communications that typically take place, in the space beside the appropriate heading (formal and/or informal).
6   For the persons with whom you typically communicate, decide how important these communications usually are to you. Next to the number of communications, for either or both the channels you have chosen, circle:

'1' if the communications are usually not at all important
'2' if they are somewhat important
'3' if they are fairly important
'4' if they are very important
'5' if they are extremely important

7   Continue this process for each person on the questionnaire for which you feel that you communicate each day.

Example

During the typical work day I usually communicate about work related matters with the following people through the:

	ID		Formal organizational structure	Informal organizational structure
Jones, Charles Clerk	2056	2	1 2 3 4 ⑤	– 1 2 3 4 5
Smith, Harry Manager	2057	5	1 2 ③ 4 5	2 1 ② 3 4 5

In this example, the person filling out the form indicated that he or she communicated twice a day with Charles Jones in business meetings or through official memos and these are extremely important to him or her. In another example, the respondent indicated that he or she typically communicated with Harry Smith about 5 times a day using formal channels and about twice a day using informal channels. In the first case the interactions were usually fairly important and in the second case only somewhat important.

Notice the last page of this form contains some blank spaces for other personnel whose names were not included in this form. If you communicate with others whose names are not on this list, please print their names, work location, and the number of formal and informal communications you usually have with them in a typical work day. Also, circle the importance of each of these interactions just as before.

Thank you for your cooperation.

The ICA communications audit and network analysis is typically carried out upon large organizations and it is therefore necessary to use relevant computer programs to generate networks from individual replies. In smaller organizations this may be done manually. The basic framework for drawing up a communication network may be outlined as follows:

Gathering information: Employees concerned are asked to mark a checklist which indicates by name or job title people with whom they communicate. Normally two basic questions are asked: 'With whom do you communicate about task/job-related matters?' 'With whom do you communicate about matters of common interest within the organization?'

In answering these questions staff are asked to indicate both the frequency of communication and its importance to them. A scale such as that indicated in the ICA instrument is often used. By using such a scale it is possible to exclude communication links below a certain level of occurrence or importance. It is also possible, if required, to exclude links that are not reciprocated.

Classifying individuals: Answers to the first question provide evidence on strictly work related communication. The following types of individual or group may be identified in this way (and by using the answers to the second question).

(a)   The 'communication star': individuals who do a large amount of communicating compared with the organizational or departmental average.

(b)   The 'clique': a group of individuals who communicate mainly with each other.

(c)   The 'bridge': a person who is a member of one communication clique and links it via a communication dyad with another clique. (A dyad is a group of two people only.)

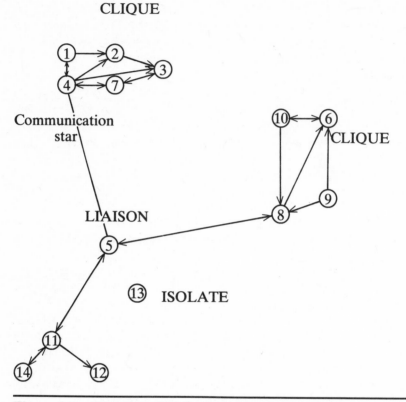

Figure 3.2   Diagram of the communications network

(d)   The 'liaison': a person who interpersonally connects two or more cliques in a system without himself/herself belonging to any clique.

(e)   The 'isolate': an individual who has relatively few communication contacts with the rest of the system.

Preparing a diagram: The information is most easily classified in a matrix chart form and is then transferred to some type of a diagrammatic form (see Figure 3.2).

Comparing charts: The network may then be compared with the formal organizational chart to see how official lines of management are reflected in actual communication behaviour. This stage may explain many problems (and prevent future ones prior to reorganization).

The grapevine: The answers to the second question provide information about the informal communication network or 'grapevine'. Studies of organizational grapevines have shown them to be sometimes inaccurate but very much faster than formal lines of communication (as they tap people's need for affiliation at work). There are clearly limits to the amount of informal communication that managers will want amongst their staff, but generally strong informal communications systems are beneficial in terms of morale. Such informal links also prove to be effective in getting the job done when formal procedures fail.

A simple network analysis of a Research Department with a project head, two secretarial staff and five research staff was carried out by a member of staff.
The organizational chart looked like this:

A   Project Head

B	C	D	E	F	G	H
(Sec)	(Sec)	(Res)	(Res)	(Res)	(Res)	(Res)

	Questions asked of:								TOTAL
	A	B	C	D	E	F	G	H	
A	–	2	2	1	0	1	0	1	7
B	2	–	10	3	2	3	5	1	26
Reported C	2	10	–	3	2	2	1	4	24
communications D	1	2	2	–	1	2	1	1	10
with: E	0	0	0	3	–	1	0	0	4
F	1	0	1	3	1	–	0	1	7
G	0	4	1	2	0	1	–	2	10
H	1	2	2	2	1	3	0	–	11
TOTAL:	7	20	18	17	7	13	7	10	

The matrix provided by answers to the question 'how often do you communicate with X about work in an average day?' is given on the previous page.

The total figures at the base of each *column* represent the number of communication events in each day in which each member of staff sees themselves taking part. The total figures at the end of each *row* represents the number of reported interactions that all other members of staff see that person as having in a typical day. Thus member of staff B sees him or herself as having a total of 20 interactions about work with other members of staff during a typical working day. On the basis of the reports from other members of staff, B typically has 26 interactions about work per day. Although these figures are substantially different it is worth noting that B is the 'communication star' of the department on both measures. (The average number of interactions per day for all staff is slightly more than 12.)

Sometimes more interesting discrepancies occur between communicating behaviour by self-report or by colleague report. For example F reports 13 communication events about work in a typical day for him or herself (i.e. equal to the average for the group). However, on the basis of the perceptions of other members of staff the same individual is seen as typically taking part in only 7 interactions per day, i.e. approximately half the departmental average. Using the above information with a suitable cut-off point (below which pairs of individuals are designated not to be communicating regularly) the following network is apparent for formal (task) communications.

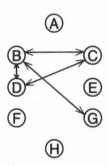

Using a similar chart and calculations for informal conversations we obtain the common interest network below:

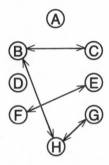

The final figure that is required prior to using the networks for analysis is the transformation of the organization chart to a form that would give some indication of predicted formal communication patterns. This is by no means always practically useful unless there is supplementary knowledge about how the different jobs in the chart relate to each other. For example, the figure below assumes an equal communication need between the manager and all his or her subordinates, regardless of whether their job is secretarial or research. Also no allowance is made for the length of communication episodes recorded.

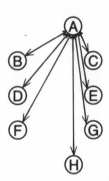

Given these communications networks the project head was able to note the differences between predicted and actual task communications behaviour and modify communications procedures accordingly.

Communication diaries

Usage

A communication diary may be kept by an individual for two purposes. The first is to provide information on the communications behaviour of the individual in his or her own right. The second is to provide information on an individual who is picked as being representative of a group, as a typical section leader or private secretary, for example.

In the former case the information will be used by the individual and/or his or her supervisor to change communication procedures or behaviour (if indicated by the information provided). In the second case the same sort of outcomes are applicable to the group of which the individual is taken to be representative. Like network analysis, communication diaries are particularly useful prior to large-scale restructuring or problem solving. They may be a logical follow-up to a network analysis, typically to be kept by those who emerge as 'communication stars' and for those who are seen to be isolates.

A manager about to launch a communications audit in his or her organization would also be well advised to keep a personal communication diary for some period. Besides providing useful information on a personal basis it will be effective in 'priming' the manager to some of the issues that will arise in the more general audit.

Organizing a Communication Diary

The amount of organization or structure required when using a communication diary as a research tool will depend upon the uses to be made of the information collected by this method. The framework described below is largely based upon ICA recommendations for use of the communication diary. Depending upon intention, auditors may choose to use a simpler or less formalized approach.

With some jobs the keeping of such a diary is somewhat of a nuisance, but for most white collar jobs a diary may be kept at a

The Techniques of Communications Auditing

Name: Steve ID#1   Date: 15 July 1975   Sheet#   1

	Communication	1	2	3	4	5	6	7	8	9	10	11	12	13	14	15
OTHER PARTY — ID# / Name																
1	Steve															
2	Helen	X														
3	Nash		X													
4	Boss			X												
5	Bill				X											
6	Dennis					X										
7	Kiwanis Club						X	X								
8	Friend								X							
9																
10																
11																
12																
13																
14																
15																
16																
17																
18																
19																
20																
21																
22																
23																
24																
25																
26																
27																
28																
29																
30																
31																
32																
Other																
INITIATOR	Self		X		X	X		X	X							
	Other	X		X			X									
CHANNEL	Face-to-face	X		X		X			X							
	Telephone		X		X											
	Written						X	X								
KIND	Job Related	X		X			X	X	X							
	Incidental (informal, nonjob related)		X			X			X							
	Organizational rumours				X											
LENGTH	Less than 3 minutes				X	X		X								
	3 to 15 minutes	X	X				X									
	15 min. to 1 hour															
	Over 1 hour			X					X							
QUALITIES	Useful	X		X			X	X								
	Extremely or very important	X		X			X	X	X							
	Fairly or very satisfactory	X			X	X			X							
	Timely															
	Accurate															

Fig. 3.3 The ICA communication diary

51

'cost' of a little more than one hour of working time per week. In a small organization it may be worthwhile to ask all employees to keep such a diary. In the larger organization various types of sampling processes are available. For example, the following may be selected:

(a) Individuals chosen as typical of their job title.
(b) A number of individuals doing the same job to see how individual variations affect communication and/or performance.
(c) Specific individuals who have been chosen for their importance within the context of the particular project.
(d) Individuals who have been shown to be worthy of investigation by prior investigation, such as network analysis. For example 'communication stars', members of specific cliques, 'isolates' and 'bridges'.

Communication diaries are kept for specified periods of time, which are determined by the project objectives and the type or volume of information they provide. A typical period might be a week.

Figure 3.3 is an example of the form used as the basis of the ICA Communication Diary, which has been filled in by a particular individual up to a certain point in his working day. This format is virtually self explanatory and may be filled in easily by an individual with the minimum interruption to his/her work. The form, if used, may be amended to suit the particular project. It is also appropriate now to add 'electronic' to the list of channels of communication.

This type of diary can yield the following information for each individual:

• Number of interactions during period surveyed
• Average number of interactions per week
• Percentage of interaction initiated by individual
• Number (and %) of face-to-face interactions
• Number (and %) of telephone calls
• Number (and %) of written communications
• Number (and %) of electronic communications
• Number (and %) of interactions less than 3 minutes
• Number (and %) of interactions between 3 and 15 minutes

- Number (and %) of interactions between 15 minutes and 1 hour
- Number (and %) of interactions over 1 hour.
- Percentage interaction classified as useful.
- Percentage interaction classified as important.
- Percentage interaction classified as satisfactory.

Averages may be obtained from all the diaries of individuals chosen as relevant and so each individual may compare his/her communications behaviour with appropriate 'norms' for the department, organization, or job type. Such diaries are also useful in providing evidence on how much communication is internal or external to chosen boundaries, e.g. department, office or total organization.

By filling in a communication diary for 6 March 1986 the author discovered that:

1   He initiated 64% of his total of 14 communication interactions.
2   86% of those interactions were face-to-face.
3   79% of the interactions were solely related to work.
4   57% were of less than 3 minutes.
    36% were of between 3 and 15 minutes.
     7% were of between 15 minutes and 1 hour.
5   The total communication time represented was 1 hour 20 minutes.
6   71% of the interactions were useful
7   14% of the interactions were very important.

Evaluating organizational telephone systems

The technology of call logging is now so advanced and relatively modest in cost that most evaluations rely heavily on call logging machines. However, other methods are applicable and useful in some circumstances. This is illustrated in the example below.

As part of an audit to investigate electronic mail systems the author carried out a survey of communications between a research centre and its funding department at the organization's head office. Staff at the centre were asked to complete record slips whenever they communicated with the head office department. This was done for letters, telephone calls, face-to-face meetings and electronic messages.

One factor that became apparent during the study was the high failure rate of telephone calls when attempting to contact specified individuals at the head office department. (A successful telephone call was defined as one in which the caller was connected to the person they wished to speak to. A half-failure was recorded when the person being sought was unavailable, but it was possible to leave a message with someone. A total failure was recorded when it was not even possible to leave a message.) The overall failure rate was 38 per cent for the period being analysed and increased to over 50 per cent at periods when a high number of telephone calls were being made. Further investigation revealed a number of potential explanations for these figures, some of which were related to the telephone system itself and some to the head office department's general procedures.

The above example illustrates a situation where a previously unnoticed fault in an organizational communication system was discovered as a consequence of an unrelated investigation. It illustrates the fact that, because individuals within an organization take particular perspectives, they may only see one part of the problem. Suitable measures to counteract this tendency range widely. Sales managers taking over in a new company may be advised to ring themselves up (from outside the company) pretending to be a customer. This simple technique can give valuable insights. At the other extreme it may be appropriate to call in a firm of consultants to evaluate the whole of the company's telecommunications systems. This type of evaluation may justify its expense by solving present-day problems, increasing efficiency, reducing costs and bringing in new communications hardware that gives a competitive edge.

Specific factors that consultants examine at the operational level of telephone usage are:

(a) How many callers encounter busy/engaged signals when trying to contact the company.

(b) The periods of maximum usage of the system and its capacity to handle average and maximum loads.

(c) Volume of workload on telephone operators and their impact on response times for incoming and outgoing calls.

(d) The age, efficiency, cost and frequency of usage of individual telephones, departmental subsystems and the organizational equipment as a whole.

(e) The implications of the usage of telephone links for computer communications.

(f) The accuracy of charges made by British Telecom for services applied.

Some aspects of telephone usage may be investigated by the manager without the aid of consultants. By use of a simple survey, based upon the telephone questionnaire shown in Figure 3.4, it is possible to obtain some useful objective and subjective feedback from employees rapidly.

Telephone call logging/monitoring/analysis

Usage

The telephone system within an organization is a corporate communication subsystem that can be differentiated out, and audited separately if a specific problem warrants such an approach. For example, if a company wishes to control rising telephone costs, either a one-off or a continuous logging exercise may be called for. Another common justification for some type of telephone monitoring exercise is that the purchase of a new telephone system is being considered. Specifically the cost and potential benefit of new and more powerful Private Automatic Branch Exchanges (PABXs) warrant careful analysis prior to any decision to buy, and may well call for expert advice from telecommunications consultants.

Telephone Questionnaire

Date ....

Name and Job Title ....

Department ....

Average usage of telephone per day:

Heavy usage (more than 25 calls)

Medium usage (15–25 calls)

Light to medium usage (5–15 calls)

Light usage (less than 5 calls)

Do you have any suggestions for improvement of the organization's telephone system?

....

....

....

Figure 3.4   Telephone questionnaire

The telephone call logger

Telephone call loggers are now common throughout the business world as adjuncts to corporate telephone systems, because of their value in two important areas: budgetary control and ensuring the efficient use of the telephone system. For the modern communications auditor they provide much information that previously had to be collected manually (and hence much more laboriously). Information on costs and types of call loggers is provided in Chapter 4. In this section a brief summary of the capabilities of such instruments will be provided so that the reader may be aware of their potential benefits. (There is a tendency to change the terminology used from 'telephone call loggers' or 'call information logging equipment' to 'telephone call management systems' as these systems have become more sophisticated.)

Such systems, it should be pointed out, do not detect and record telephone conversations. They do monitor all other activities on exchange lines, extensions and private circuits. A call logger attached to PABX can record:

● The time, date and duration of each call.
● Dialled numbers.
● The extension from which the call has been made.
● The cost of each call.
● The time that incoming callers have to wait before their call is answered.
● The number of incoming callers who do not wait until the call is answered.

This information may be used in various ways to increase efficiency of telephone usage or allocate costs on a budgeting basis. For example:

(a) Printouts can be given immediately of calls which exceed certain predetermined parameters (e.g. calls costing more than £2, international calls, calls that last more than one hour).
(b) Costs may be summarized for peak, standard or off-peak calls.
(c) Costs may be allocated by department to allow efficient calculation of overheads and variable costs
(d) Information can be provided to indicate the degree of use of

each extension, which may point out some extensions which do not justify their rental charges.

(e) The 'busy hour' for the exchange may be identified: internal users may be asked to avoid placing calls at this peak time so that incoming calls from customers may be served more efficiently.

A survey was carried out in four central government departments to evaluate the cost-effectiveness of telephone extension logging. In this study call logging techniques showed up an over-provision in exchange lines of 10 per cent or more and in extensions of 20 per cent or more and potential savings in call charge costs of 20–30 per cent. The total potential savings identified were £135,000 per year. The pay-back time for the purchase, maintenance and running costs of extension logging was estimated to be less than three years.

A communications audit, carried out for British Telecom by Bristol Polytechnic staff, of communication patterns in local authorities used telephone call logging as a technique. Temporary installation of call logging machines at two sites within a district council provided the following information:

(a) A comparison of telephone bills derived from call logging versus actual bills from British Telecom for both sites.

(b) A breakdown of all incoming and outgoing calls by duration of call.

(c) Totals of incoming and outgoing calls from each site for each half-hour during the working day.

(d) A matrix showing frequency of all internal calls between the 17 departments within one site and a similar matrix for the 10 departments at the other site.

(e) A selected destination matrix for external calls from each site.

In-tray Out-tray analysis

Usage

This is a technique that can be used to classify documentary communications received and sent by individuals.
Conceptually it forms a subsection of the communication diary, although it may be used as a stand-alone
device. It is primarily used to allow individuals (sometimes representative of groups with the same task in the
company) to obtain a quantitative indication of the type
and size of paper traffic they process as part of their job.

Carrying out an In-tray Out-tray analysis

The first step is to specify the objective of the exercise and then
design appropriate charts or forms. Examples of such forms are
given in Figures 3.5 and 3.6.

After filling in forms for all documents received and sent over a
suitably representative period it will typically be possible to:

(a) Calculate how much of your time you spend on reading and
     writing documents, as a proportion of your working day.
(b) Establish which individuals and departments you communi-
     cate with most frequently (in writing).
(c) Decide which types of document you should arrange not to
     receive in future.
(d) Begin to decide which documentary communications systems
     within the organization require modification.
(e) Decide whether you are any of the following:

     ● 'Information sink'
     ● 'Document hoarder'
     ● 'Information generator'
     ● 'Paper processor'

In the wider context this technique is useful in helping to
improve individual time management and efficiency.

In-tray analysis

Name and organization/department of sender:

. . . .

Document title and/or brief description:

. . . .

Length of document (pages): . . . .

Time taken to deal with document (i.e. reading and actions required as a consequence of its receipt)

. . . .

Was the document: Useful?   ☐
(Please tick any   Important?   ☐
relevant box)   Inappropriate?   ☐

After reading the document did you: Pass it on?   ☐
                                     Retain it?   ☐
                                     Take a copy of it? ☐

Please specify any actions you had to take as a consequence of receipt of the document (other than the above).

. . . .

. . . .

. . . .

Comments . . . .

Figure 3.5 In-tray analysis form

Out-tray analysis

Destination(s) of document (Name and oganization/department):

. . . .

Document title and/or brief description: . . . .

. . . .

Length of document (pages): . . . .

Time taken to prepare document . . . .

Comments: . . . .

. . . .

. . . .

Figure 3.6 Out-tray analysis form

Other useful techniques in communications auditing

The techniques described so far have been chosen because they are widely used by consulting communications auditors and are suitable for use by managers wishing to carry out audits in their own organizations. The techniques described in the next sections are likely to be of use to the do-it-yourself auditor, although they are not so widely used by consultants in the field. They are:

- The Fog Index.
- The 'original' communications audit.
- The critical incident technique.

The Fog Index

> **Usage**
>
> The Fog Index was developed in the 1940s by Robert Gunning, a writer and editor in the USA, as a measure of readability. It tells the writer of an article or document the number of years of education that a reader needs to have had in order to understand the particular message, and can be used to assess the clarity of business communications for target audiences. The Fog Index may be used to evaluate any type of written document used either within an organization or outside it (when communicating with clients or the public at large). Similarly the individual writer can evaluate his or her own written communications.

Calculating the Fog Index of a document consists of a number of steps.

1   Select a representative passage from the document.
2   Count out 100 words. The sample passage ends at the end of the sentence nearest to 100 words from the start of the sample passage.
3   Record the number of words in the sample passage (somewhere around 100).
4   Determine the average number of words per sentence in the sample passage by dividing the total number of words by the number of sentences.
5   Count the number of 'difficult' words in the passage. These are defined as those with three or more syllables. Three-syllable words not counted as difficult are compound words such as bookkeeper and verbs whose third syllable is 'ed' or 'es'.
6   Add the average number of words in a sentence to the number of difficult words in the passage.
7   Multiply this total by 0.4.
8   The resulting number is the number of years of education needed by the audience to understand the passage, i.e. the Fog Index.

Putting this as a formula:

Fog Index = 0.4 $(x + y)$

where x = average number of words per sentence
y = number of 'difficult' words.

[It may be necessary to select a number of passages in the case of longer documents to be sure that a representative figure has been achieved.]

It has been found that almost all audiences prefer to read well below their education levels and so when there is a serious intention to communicate the calculation of the Fog Index is worthwhile. Popular magazines in the UK are said to have a Fog Index of about 6. Newspapers in the UK have Fog Indexes varying from about 10 to about 14. There is evidence to suggest that even those with a PhD will not spend prolonged periods reading material with a Fog Index of over 13. Analysis of business communications, however, shows them to be frequently in the range of 17 to 20.

The Fog Index is the best known of a variety of measures of readability that are simple and easy to apply. Two factors need to be noted when using it:

1   Achieving a low Fog Index does not itself imply that documentation is readable, as the effective removal of communication barriers is not simply a matter of using simple words and short sentences. Jargon, for example, can prevent communication and will not necessarily create a high Fog Index when included in text.

2   There are some occasions when a high Fog Index cannot be easily avoided, when writing about 'auditing organizational communications' for example. With topics such as this one has at least some excuse for the Fog Index of 19 in parts of the text!

The DHSS and other government departments as well as large private organizations have been taking steps to make their communications with the public more comprehensible in recent years.

In the USA the Internal Revenue Service has been using the Fog Index for years to evaluate its written communications. In spite of this it appears that income tax forms still sometimes contain sentences with as many as 54 words. It appears, therefore, that 'one can guide an equine quadruped to aqueous liquid and yet not induce him to imbibe'. Or alternatively 'you can lead a horse to water but you can't make him drink'.

The 'original' communications audit

The first widely quoted reference to the term 'communications audit' is an article about the use of such a technique by G.S.Odiorne in 1954. The article concerned described the use of a simple questionnaire in a US research and development corporation dealing in electronic devices. Because of personnel problems Odiorne carried out research in the organization to investigate communications and other related matters. As a first stage the audit questionnaire was presented to a top management group of ten. They were instructed to answer the questions in terms of the research engineers who worked for them. That is, the items in the audit were preceded by the following statement: 'Most of the engineers in the lower echelon group will answer these questions as follows'. The second stage was to ask 30 such project engineers to answer the questions for themselves. Figure 3.7 is a copy of the audit question and the results (actual and managerial predictions). Figure 3.8 represents typical answers to the more open question.

In the particular situation this method was clearly effective in illustrating some serious discrepancies between the views of managers and their subordinate engineers. Question 8 particularly highlights this point.

Although this is a rather more general questionnaire it may well be a useful starting point for managers wishing to 'test the water' in relation to their own subordinates. It would form a useful structured questionnaire in itself or might be incorporated into one more appropriate to a particular company.

> 'When they were setting up, they got us all together to talk about what power tools would be best all round. Then they put in the ones we agreed on. I've never seen anything like it in all the years I've been in engineering.'
>
> Nissan Worker, County Durham

QUESTION	SUMMARY OF ANSWERS				
	Management's Prediction		Engineers' Answers		
	Yes	No	Yes	No	Other
1 Do you feel that you are a part of management?	20	10	24	3	3
2 Do you feel that you have a part in management planning?	2	28	12	15	3
3 Do you feel that you are adequately informed on management aims and long range planning?	26	4	5	25	0
4 What management information would you like to receive?	omitted		see Table 2		
5 Do you think that present information channels are adequate?	29	1	5	23	2
6 What suggestions do you have to improve present meetings?	omitted		see Table 2		
7 Is there enough management participation in departmental meetings?	26	4	8	14	8
8 Would you like to participate more in company planning?	3	27	27	3	1
9 Is your authority commensurate with your responsibility?	26	4	20	9	1
10 Do you feel free to seek counsel on special problems related to but not part of your job?	30	0	25	5	0
11 Do you feel closer to the people you supervise than to the people who supervise you?	9	21	12	5	13
12 Are promotions given generally to proper and deserving individuals?	28	2	18	8	4
13 Do you receive proper tools, information, and incentives to function as part of management?	2	28	8	17	5
14 Is cooperation and contact with other departments satisfactory?	15	15	19	7	4
15 Does management inform you adequately about the industry, the company, products, financial standing, and proposed changes?	29	1	6	23	1
16 How could your work be made more effective?	omitted		see Table 2		

Figure 3.7   Results of the 'original' communications audit

Summaries of Answers to Questions 4, 6, 7, and 16 of the Communications Audit

Summary of Answers to Question 4

WHAT MANAGEMENT INFORMATION WOULD YOU LIKE TO RECEIVE?

The majority concern themselves with long range planning, management aims, and detailed information about the company. Some typical comments in reply to this question were:

'More info' regarding growth, future of the business, and plans for expansion in new fields.'
'I'd like reports on contracts, financial reports, and how much money the company is making.'
'I'd like more reports on how my department is doing, how the delivered product was accepted. Even complaints if it didn't pan out a year later. Maybe a *well done* if it is really deserved.'
'More dope on policies, and expected changes.'

Summary of Answers to Question 6

WHAT SUGGESTIONS DO YOU HAVE TO IMPROVE PRESENT MEETINGS?

Some typical comments included the following:

'What meetings?'
'More of them, and better representation by the people who really know what is going on in each department or project, not just the guy who can be spared best from his job because he's useless anyhow.'
'Circulate the agenda in advance, and then do something about it when everybody agrees on the right course.'
'Have some first.'
'Put them on a planned basis, issue an agenda, and issue minutes afterward so everybody will know what came out of them.'
'Attach a few penalites to failure to attend, especially the principal people involved. They don't show up, then yell bloody murder if they aren't consulted over some move.'
'The boss should keep his mouth shut until after somebody else has had a chance to say something. That kills the discussion every time.'

Summary of Answers to Question 7

IS THERE ENOUGH MANAGEMENT PARTICIPATION IN DEPARTMENT MEETINGS?

'I don't know that such meetings are held.'
'Too damn much when held,'
'They don't come themselves, they just send the accountants or personnel guys around to listen in to what is going on.'
'Probably a lot more than is required.'

Figure 3.8 Answers to open questions in 'original' communications audit

Summary of Answers to Question 16

HOW COULD YOUR WORK BE MADE MORE EFFECTIVE?

'More appreciation for each job—I mean they should form more of a team.'

'More space, more secretarial help, and less harassment from accountants and ribbon clerks.'

'More criticism of the project's efficiency, and a good word or a raise when something really outstanding is accomplished.'

'Consult with project engineers before committing the company to a project. This applies not only to budgets, which are set by non-project persons, but to technical stuff too,'

'Quit treating us like hired brain-boxes. They think they can just throw any problem there's a profit in to us and we're supposed to sink or swim.'

'Get rid of some of this non-engineering work. Let the man with the degree work at the things he's trained for, and hire helpers and train them for the rest of it.'

'Willingness to listen to a qualified technical opinion without going stuffed shirt and phony executive on us.'

Figure 3.8 (concluded)

Critical incident technique

> **Usage**
>
> This technique is particularly useful in obtaining evidence from staff on the most common (or memorable) communication problems in the organization. It also provides information on good communications practices.

The technique is a well established one that has been shown to be an effective research tool in many areas. In this particular context employees are asked to describe critical communication episodes which they feel are representative of typical successful or unsuccessful incidents. From the descriptions it is possible to understand and illustrate why departments or organizations are having communication problems. Figure 3.9 shows the author's adaptation of one used by the ICA in the United States for recording critical communication incidents.

In using this form some method of 'priming' the respondent is called for. If it is one technique in the middle of a wider communication audit this 'priming' will already have occurred. If it is the first

Please try to think of a recent work-related experience of yours in which communication was particularly ineffective or effective. Please answer the questions below relating to the experience.

A.   To whom does this experience primarily relate?
    1   A subordinate   2   A co-worker
    3   An immediate supervisor 4   A Senior manager.

B.   Was the quality of communication:
    1   Effective?   2   Ineffective?

C.   Describe the communication experience, the circumstances leading up to it, what the person did that made him/her an effective or ineffective communicator, and the results or outcome of what the person did. Thank you.

. . . .

. . . .

. . . .

. . . .

. . . .

Figure 3.9 Communications Audit Communicative Experience Form

step, then a few spoken words of introduction are called for, taking care however not to bias the potential replies by pointing people in a particular direction. It should also be noted that respondents are likely to remember ineffective communication experiences more than effective ones. Hence, if this type of reply predominates this does not *necessarily* imply poor communications with the organization.

The author tested the form in Figure 3.9 upon a small number of people relating to their communications with various organizations. The following issues in communication emerged.

Respondent 1 reports failure to resolve a routine question about use of computers due to differing preconceptions and understanding of the problem by the persons involved.

Respondent 2 reports failure of a colleague to read and act upon a simple message sent in an internal memo . The outcome was extra work for the respondent, and the reduced standing in his estimation of the colleague following the experience.

Respondent 3 reports an unsatisfactory episode where a supervisor took disagreement on a factual matter as a challenge to her authority and this prevented effective communication.

Respondent 4 reports having formally requested in writing the correction of a fault in a financial system six times over a period of 2 years without success.

Respondent 5 reports having to do a job rapidly and consequently ineffectively as a consequence of his boss not having passed on relevant information at the appropriate time.

Summary

This chapter has provided details and examples of communications auditing techniques likely to be of value to a manager wishing to carry out a do-it-yourself audit in his or her own company. The techniques covered were:

- Problem definition
- Unstructured interviews
- Structured interviews
- Self-completion questionnaires (also known as postal questionnaires)

- Group discussions
- Network analysis (also known as socio-grams)
- Communication diaries
- Telephone call logging
- In-tray/Out-tray analysis
- The Fog Index
- The 'original' communications audit
- Critical incident technique

Managers will need to use the problem definition technique in all communications audits, but the particular objectives of the audit will decide which other techniques are called for.

In the case of some of the techniques further reading may be useful and the following books are recommended in this context:

Survey Research Practice by Hoinville and Jowell (Heinemann, London 1978) provides a readable and comprehensive description of interviews, questionnaires and group discussions.

Auditing Organizational Communication Systems: The ICA Communication Audit by Goldhaber and Rogers (Kendall/ Hunt, Dubuque 1979) provides a detailed description of its title topic. Techniques used include interviews and questionnaires, critical incidents, network analysis and the communication diary.

The Technique of Clear Writing by Gunning (McGraw-Hill, New York 1952) describes the Fog Index in the words of its inventor.

4 Communications equipment

The different means of communication that organizational members can use today have been available for greatly varying lengths of time. Spoken face-to-face communications were arguably a prerequisite for the initiation of the first organization. Telephones have been with us for the lesser time of approximately a century. Mobile cellular telephones have been generally obtainable for only a few years.

In looking at communications equipment in this chapter we shall be concentrating upon the developments of the last few years, in order to alert readers to the ways that have recently become available to improve communications efficiency. The rapid strides that have been made in telecommunications capability recently increase the chances that systems already installed in companies are out of date. Ten years ago companies changed their telephone switchboards roughly once every fifteen years, now it is more than once every seven years.

The increased rate of change in telecommunications (and computing) means it is very easy to become submerged in a sea of data that makes decisions on this issue very difficult. This adds to the more traditional difficulty associated with trying to decide between competing suppliers of equipment. A further complication is the convergence of telecommunications and computing.

In order to clarify issues in this area, in this chapter we shall look at equipment in terms of facilities provided; that is, taking an approach that allows the individual manager to decide what facilities are needed for the organization. This will be followed up by a look at the capabilities available in present-day equipment.

Here is a summary of the equipment/systems currently available in terms of the facilities they provide.

Telephone	The facility to communicate orally over long distances
Cellular mobile telephone	The facility to communicate orally over long distances away from conventional fixed telephones (typically from moving vehicles).
Teleconferencing	The facility to communicate orally (and possibly visually) over long distances with a number of people simultaneously.
Telephone call logger	The facility to monitor and analyse telephone calls continuously.
Answering machines	The facility to have telephone messages recorded and stored whilst no one is available to answer the telephone.
Telex	The facility to transmit small amounts of text rapidly from one location to another.
Teletex	The facility to transmit larger amounts of text more rapidly and accurately from one location to another.
Facsimile (or Fax)	The facility to send images (including text) from one location to another by means of ordinary telephone lines.
Electronic mail (E-Mail)	The facility to send text between electronic devices and have it printed out or displayed on screens. Also includes the facility to store messages.
Local Area Network (LAN)	The facilities provided by the linking up of the computers at a single location.

Wide Area Network (WAN)	The facilities provided by linking up computers over longer distances.
Viewdata (also known as Interactive videotex)	The facility to use a visual display unit as a terminal connected to a computer database over the telephone network. (Prestel is an example of this type of system.)
PABX (Private Automatic Branch Exchange)	The central core of the organizational telephone/ telecommunications system which is a vital element for many of the above systems.
Acoustic coupler	A device which offers the facility to send computer signals by means of the public telephone system. (The telephone receiver is physically fitted into it to provide this facility.)
Modem	A device which offers the facility to send computer signals by means of the public telephone system, which bypasses the handset. (It allows information to be sent more rapidly and reliably than when an acoustic coupler is used.)

The rest of this chapter is devoted to an examination of these facilities within the context of equipment that is currently available.

Telephones

Telephones are now commonly seen as part of organizational systems and it is difficult to cut the system into discrete parcels for analysis. However, some boundaries need to be drawn and so this section will be largely limited to describing recent developments in telephone handsets.

The most obvious physical changes that have occurred in such handsets over recent years are in their size, weight, colour and the fact that they have pushbuttons rather than circular rotating dials.

It is not obviously apparent how the first three features can significantly improve communication; in fact, the lower weight can be a distinct disadvantage. With some modern telephones the elasticity of the wire can easily pull the base of the set across and off the desk if the user leans back in his chair whilst making a call! The pushbutton feature is more obviously useful, in that the dialling process is more rapid and less prone to mistakes, although calls are not actually connected any faster.

A less obvious change is that a larger part of the set is now sensitive to sound waves. In older sets it was possible to put one's hand over the mouthpiece when wishing to say something to someone other than the caller without the latter hearing. On new telephones the whole receiver is sound sensitive and so unguarded remarks may be picked up by the person at the other end of the line.

Most new telephones now have a last number redial facility; if the number dialled is engaged it is possible to call it later without having to punch in the whole number again. More sophisticated handsets have a number memory capacity that is useful if one calls a fairly large repertoire of numbers regularly. Also available are incorporated digital displays showing the number being called and acting as a clock and call-timer.

The telephone that offers on-the-hook dialling is becoming more widely used and is particularly useful when frequently dialling numbers that take a long time to answer. These telephones provide a ringing tone through a microphone so that one knows when to lift the receiver. Cordless telephones are also available for those who need to move round a limited area and wish to take the telephone with them.

More sophisticated facilities are available when the telephone handset is part of one of the modern systems available, such as the British Telecom Merlin Phone System. Such systems are provided by a variety of manufacturers for businesses of any size and typically offer at least the following capabilities of the system user:

(a)   Individual extensions may be 'gated' so that they cannot be used for certain types of calls, e.g. long-distance or overseas calls.

(b)   Call logging.

(c)   Diversion of calls from one extension to another more convenient one (useful if you are working in another office for a time).

(d)   Diversion of calls to another extension if the call is not answered after a specified number of rings.
(e)   Automatic redialling of continuously engaged numbers.
(f)   Call transfer directly between extensions.

There are further comments about new telephone capabilities appear in the later section on PABXs.

Cellular mobile telephones

Cellular mobile telephones are car-based or completely portable telephones which are connected to the standard British Telecom telephone network via a network of radio transmitters (each of which covers a 'cell' of the country). Using these 'cellphones' it is possible to make local, national and international calls (typically from a car) just as one would make a call from an ordinary static telephone.

There are two cellular operators, Cellnet and Vodafone, and they have roughly equal market shares. At the time of writing the two systems, which are less than two years old, are suffering some problems because demand is running at around twice the predictions. This means that at some peak times, in the London area especially, there are not enough channels available to take all the calls that users are trying to put through.

The advanced cellular telephones have similar features to static telephones. These include a memory, on-hook dialling, illuminated keypads, a fluorescent display of the number being dialled, and an electronic lock to prevent unauthorized use. They also offer additional features such as:

(a)   'Call forward': the capacity to redirect incoming calls to a chosen number.
(b)   'No-answer transfer': automatic redirection of calls to a designated number if there is no answer.
(c)   'Conference call': allows three-way conversations.
(d)   'Call waiting': indication of another call on the line, and the capacity to answer it whilst keeping the original call on hold.
(e)   The option to purchase 'bolt on' extras that give the capacity to send computer data over the cellular telephone.

Besides the cost of purchase and installation of the cellular telephone the user has to pay a system-joining fee, and a monthly subscription charge to be connected to the network. On top of this, the cost of calls from (and *to*) cellular telephones is substantially higher than that for static telephones.

A survey of the users of cellular phones in 1985 showed them to be largely people running their own small businesses. Typical users in this survey were estate agents and plumbers. At the same time the system operators were aiming their marketing at wholesalers, utilities such as gas and electricity, and the construction industry.

For the user who requires a completely mobile telephone, there are models that do not have to be installed in a car. These can be easily carried around in a briefcase, although it is necessary to recharge the batteries occasionally. People who travel regularly by train can use trainphones on an increasing number of Pullman services and on the express services between Victoria and Gatwick Airport.

Teleconferencing

Teleconferencing is a fast cost-effective way of convening meetings with colleagues and clients in the UK or abroad. The people involved stay at their own base location and meet via telephone links, thus saving the time, money and energy spent in travelling to a distant meeting. This capability has two variants: audioconferencing and videoconferencing. Both of these variants may be supplemented by the use of fax (facsimile) transmission and an 'electronic blackboard'. This latter feature involves a 'white board' at one end which, when drawn upon, displays an image on a screen at the other end.

Audioconferencing is the simpler form of teleconferencing, allowing a conference by telephone with up to twenty people at different locations. The organizer books the conference in advance via the British Telecom operator (or international operator if the conference involves international calls). To carry out the booking it is necessary only to specify the time and date of the conference, and give each party's telephone number. Just before the appointed time the organizer is called and advised the conference is about to be set up. This then involves the operator contacting each member of the audioconference and connecting them to the bridging equipment. The 'conference' then proceeds. Facsimile transmission may be used to enhance the audioconference so that papers can be circulated by the organizer to those taking part.

Videoconferencing has the same capability with the addition of a video link, which allows participants to see each other as well as hearing each other. It can be organized using a British Telecom videoconferencing room or by using a private terminal set up within the user's organization. A typical videoconferencing room provided by British Telecom accommodates up to six participants, but additional personnel can be included if necessary.

Videoconferencing can be enhanced by:

(a)   The use of a display facility for documents and diagrams.
(b)   Facsimile transfer of paperwork between locations.
(c)   Full recording of the meeting.
(d)   'Overflow' capacity which allows other groups to listen in.

Telephone call logging

The telephone call logger has already been discussed in the previous chapter on communications auditing techniques. Further brief comments made in this section should be read in conjunction with this earlier section.

When call loggers are used as an analysis or consultancy tool it is logical to hire them for the short time required for the particular auditing exercise. Increasingly, however, the call logger is being seen as a useful continuous monitor, in view of its potential for reducing telephone costs or allocating them to particular departments. This usage calls for purchase rather than short term hire. Costs vary according to the model and the number of telephone lines being monitored. At 1985 prices the cost of a single-line call logger varied between £100 and £400. Systems that can monitor exchanges carrying multiple lines for small to medium-sized organizations cost between £300 and £4,500. For the large organization with a 150-line exchange, costs for a logging system are of the order of £7,500. The loggers at this top end of the market need to be more sophisticated than the single-line loggers, but their cost per line is in fact less than that of the single-line loggers.

Answering machines

Answering machines have been with us for a long time, but they are worth mentioning briefly, because modern microprocessor-controlled versions now available are much more sophisticated than older models. Modern machines (which may incorporate their own telephone handset) have many of the new capabilities described in the earlier section on telephones. In addition they are able to:

(a)   display the number of messages waiting.
(b)   allow recording of important conversations when using the integral telephone.
(c)   automatically diagnose their own faults and indicate them.
(d)   allow you to activate remote replay of messages from any other phone by use of a prearranged voice code.

A more recent innovation in this area is voice mail. Under this system individuals ringing a number and finding it engaged or unanswered can elect to post their intended message into a computer 'mailbox'. When the would-be recipient returns he or she can ring their mailbox and retrieve any waiting messages. Voice mail systems are based upon computers that are attached to the company's PABX. The caller's messages are converted into digital form and stored in the computer memory. When replayed they retain their original tone and inflexion. As well as this basic function, more sophisticated voice mail systems can offer extra facilities, such as preprogrammed multiple mailing of messages to a number of recipients simultaneously.

Telex

Telex provides fast 'written' communication to almost any part of the world (providing the addressee is linked to the telex system). The message is typed into the machine at the sending point and is received and typed out at the destination point within seconds. This messaging system has been in existence for over 50 years and is still growing at a rate of about 15 per cent per year. Estimates vary as to the number of subscribers worldwide, but it is somewhere in the $1\frac{1}{2}$ to 2 million range.

The system has the advantage that messages can be sent at any time of the day or night, and will be received automatically by the addressee's machine. Because of the speed of the message it is possible for two users to have a text-based 'conversation'.

Compared with more recently developed systems, telex now suffers from a relative slowness in terms of amount of information transmitted per unit time and low quality of communication. Modern telex machines, however, have some word-processing capacity and automatic sending facilities. Besides cost of purchase or rental of the machine a leased line is also required.

Owners of microcomputers can now buy peripherals which provide a telex facility. Also electronic mail systems now provide telex capability by direct connections between the two networks. It is likely that telex will be increasingly superseded in the future by faster and cheaper electronic mail systems. However, the large number of telex terminals currently installed worldwide make the telex interface a useful feature for microcomputers, word processors and local area networks.

Teletex

Teletex should not be confused with the similar sounding teletext, which is the public television system behind Oracle and Ceefax. Teletex is a new text communications service that transmits letter quality documents between terminals, such as electronic typewriters and word processors.

Teletex was developed from West German government-supported research into methods of improving text communications. It is text-oriented, more reliable, cheaper and faster than telex. (Through an exchange facility teletex users can also send messages to the telex system.) It has a larger character set than telex, is essentially error free and allows faithful reproduction of documents, with format, layout, spacing and graphics characters identical in the transmitted and received documents. Teletex also has fully automatic transmission, receipt and acknowledgement of documents, together with error detection and correction procedures.

One of the main objectives of the teletex system is to improve compatibility between organizations wishing to transmit/receive text. Thus options available for potential teletex users are:

● Purpose-built terminals for teletex similar in design to teleprinters, but with full text editing capability and larger storage capacity.
● Word processors and microcomputers capable of acting as teletex terminals.

- Communicating typewriters. These are mainly electronic type-writers modified by adding communication modules and floppy discs to handle teletex messages.
- Teletex adaptors, i.e. 'black box devices' that can connect intelligent terminals, such as word processors and microcomputers, to the network.

Teletex has yet to catch on to any great degree due to stiff competition from other new methods of communication, and the presence of the well-established, but inferior, telex system.

Facsimile or fax

Fax is a way of sending an exact copy of text and documents containing graphic material in black and white to another fax user over the telephone network. A fax machine scans documents and transmits signals which are then converted by the receiving fax machine to the original form. Fax machines are said to be as easy to operate as a photocopier, but the system is faster than telex: the contents of an A4 page can be transmitted to anyone in the world in 20 seconds. (There are four fax standards based upon the speed of transmission of an A4 sheet; 20 seconds represents the fastest standard currently available.) Like telex it does not require a receiving operator and modern machines have various automatic features to save time. Fax can handle handwritten notes, drawings and diagrams, in fact anything that a photocopier can reproduce.

Earlier compatibility problems have been resolved and so growth in fax usage is increasing, especially overseas. Fax has over 50,000 UK users and is used in over 90 countries.

Electronic mail

Electronic mail is a system which passes information electronically from sender to receiver. In its broadest sense this definition includes telex, teletex and fax. The factor which differentiates the common usage of the term today from the wider sense is the incorporation of an electronic mailbox on a central computer. This central computer is the core of the system and ensures that a user/subscriber can send, receive and collect waiting messages from suitably linked terminals anywhere within the electronic mail network. Messages can be stored in the mailbox for as long as is required.

A recent survey in the UK has shown that most electronic messaging is done within companies. However, in small to medium-sized organizations electronic mail is most likely to be used for communication with other organizations through systems such as Telecom Gold or Prestel. As company size increases, or when geographical dispersion of locations occurs, internal mail becomes more important. It is estimated that there are more than 50,000 UK electronic mail users at the time of writing, excluding the local in-house systems.

Electronic mailboxes are very useful for people who move from office to office and need to pick up messages at different times of day and from different locations. (They include the facility to connect by portable terminal from any telephone.) Another great advantage of electronic mail is that users do not have to worry about compatibility. Most modern office equipment – electronic typewriters, word processors, personal computers, viewdata terminals and, in some cases, telex machines – can send and receive electronic messages with the addition of a modem and some software. Consequently, this reduces start-up costs in comparison to telex or teletex. Finally, electronic mail is cheap and rapid.

Local area networks

One of the key concepts in communications systems today is that of *convergence* (i.e. the convergence of communications and computers). This means that it is becoming increasingly difficult to discuss communications without a substantial overlap into the field of computing. The local area network (or LAN) is one manifestation of this overlap. The LAN is the mechanism by which the computers on a single site are linked up. Although LANs have been around for some time (ten years at the time of writing) interest in them has increased recently, not least because of the influx of microcomputers into organizations. Users of these microcomputers have realized that their capabilities, although substantial, are limited when they are used in isolation. This may be confirmed by looking at tasks that are carried out in organizations.

Most tasks call for information from other departments at some stage in order to achieve the objectives in hand. Normally after the task has been carried out information obtained has to be passed on to others, in the form of reports, etc. By networking the micro-computers together (into a local area network) this communications aspect of the job can be achieved much more efficiently. A second factor that encourages networking is its usefulness in facilitating the 'electronic office', which seeks to improve productivity by the use of electronic mail, and other recent alternatives to the conventional paper-based office systems.

Local area networks include mainframe and minicomputers as well as micros and also allow the sharing of more expensive equipment, such as printers. LANs have a number of feasible topologies such as:

1 A 'star' network, where all the stations are linked to one central controller.
2 A 'ring' network, where all the devices are connected by a continuous ring.
3 A 'bus' arrangement, where devices are connected to the branches of a central spine.

By efficient planning at the initial installation stage it is possible for the network to grow as demands change with time.

An alternative to the conventional local area network is becoming available with PABXs that use digital (rather than analogue) circuits. This alternative uses the PABX and the associated telephone system as the core of the network. The PABX-based system is slower, but offers advantages in terms of ready-made connections with the public telephone networks. There is also a potential saving on installation in that the ducting (and possibly cabling) required is already in place.

Wide area networks

Wide area networks (WANs) connect together computer equipment over wider areas than local area networks, possibly over an entire country, or worldwide. This can be achieved, for example, through the British Telecom Packet SwitchStream system (PSS) which was designed specifically for computer-based information. Alternatively, there is the British Telecom Datel service, which provides a means of transmitting data through the public telephone network.

Other alternatives are entirely private systems that involve the leasing of private lines from British Telecom, or the use of Value Added Network systems that are not part of British Telecom.

Viewdata or videotex

Videotex is a general term for interactive communication systems carrying text or graphics over telephone lines or cables. In the UK these are also called viewdata. The UK public access viewdata system is known as Prestel; there are also private viewdata systems.

Viewdata systems give access to information stored on a central computer database. Transmission may be (a) by television broadcasting, i.e. the Ceefax and Oracle services, or (b) over a telephone line or cable. Only the latter will be dealt with in this section in view of its business orientation. The terminal used can be a conventional television set with an adaptor containing a modem to link it to the telephone system. Also required is a keyboard having at least the figures 0 to 9 and the star and square symbols. Alternatively, a microcomputer with appropriate software can be used. A printer is also needed if hard copy of selected pages is required.

The terminal will automatically call up the central computer containing the database when the appropriate button on the keyboard is pressed; logging on to the computer is also automatic. The database consists of 'pages' of information supplied by Information Providers. The pages are linked in a 'tree' structure. Access is designed to be as simple as possible and does not require training, although it may be tedious at times. The first page that is seen, on access to the system, has a 'menu' with a number of further page choices. After one of these has been chosen a page from the next level down is displayed with a further menu. This process continues through the 'tree' structure until the page with the required information is reached. Alternatively, it is possible to call up the page directly if the required page number is known. The Prestel service largely provides information oriented towards the business community, and is ideal for those users seeking information that needs constant updating, such as share prices. More general information is also provided relating to news, weather, entertainment, etc. Figure 4.1 shows typical pages from Prestel.

P R E S T E L   56a   Op
Business
1 PRESTEL CITISERVICE
  Continuously updated prices,news,
  commentaries,recommendations & charts
  on all financial & money markets,the
  Stock Exchange,unit trusts &
  insurance funds;stockbrokers'
  research databases & electronic
  dealing services

2 BUSINESS INFORMATION
  Business News,Financial & Economic
  Information,Shipping, & information
  provided by Government Departments.
  Company information & credit
  management services

7 BANKING   8 COMPANY INFORMATION
9 INSURANCE   0 MAIN INDEX

P R E S T E L   1877a   Op
Small firms
1 SMALL FIRMS SERVICE Help from
  Department of Trade & Industry
2 EXPORT ADVISORY SERVICE A guide to
  for small businesses without export
  experience
3 TENDERING FOR GOVERNMENT CONTRACTS
  Advice for small firms

9 COMPANY INFORMATION
0 MAIN EMPLOYMENT INDEX

Figure 4.1 **Typical pages from Prestel**

Dept Trade & Industry   2041a   Op

The Government's objective is to create
an economic climate in which industry
can expand and prosper.
Firms can get help from the Govt for
industrial investment in several ways,
usually an outright cash grant or a
loan at a favourable rate of interest.

that you should consult the particular
Dept responsible for the help you need
before you commit yourself to spending
money on any project.

Key _ to continue
          ·0 main index

Dept Trade & Industry   20416a   Op

If you're running a small business or
want to start one, the Small Firms
Service can help with 'how to do it'
and with problems when they arise.

To get in touch with the Service,
dial 100 and ask the operator for
----------Freefone Enterprise----------

Note   Responsibility for the Small
Firms Service was transferred to the
Department of Employment on 3 September
1985.

          0 aid to industry index

Figure 4.1   (concluded)

Besides providing information Prestel has other services available:

(a) *Response frames*. Information providers (IPs) can include pages which allow the user to make some kind of 'response'. For example, this may be a page requesting a brochure, or making a reservation or a purchase. The response frame is then 'sent' to the IP by the system.
(b) *Mailbox*. Messages can be sent to other users to be seen by them when they next log on. Users with only numeric keypads have to restrict themselves to standard messages (e.g. greetings). Users with full alphanumeric keyboards can compose their own messages. It is also possible to send telex messages via Prestel.
(c) *Gateway*. Gateway allows Prestel users to gain access to third-party computer systems via special pages. (The closed user group facility allows access to some pages to be restricted to certain users only.) This facility is used for example, to allow travel agents to make bookings on ferries, to allow home computer users to receive software over the telephone line, and to allow users in certain areas to order their groceries.

The costs of the Prestel service to users are made up of:

(a) The cost of the telephone call.
(b) A time charge (except in the evenings and at weekends at the time of writing).
(c) A quarterly subscription charge.
(d) The cost of an appropriate terminal or software.

Private viewdata is an attractive format for private information retrieval systems where users are not computer experts. Essentially, private viewdata systems are the same as Prestel, except that they allow access to and interaction with specific information rather faster. They are designed exclusively for business use and are sold complete to business users who run them on their own central computers. (Alternatively, computer bureaux run private viewdata systems which they manage on behalf of corporate users.) Private viewdata only becomes cost-effective when there is a need to keep large numbers of staff in touch with a head office and in contact with the central computer. They therefore have greater potential for large, rather than small/medium, organizations.

Private automatic branch exchanges (PABXs)

The telephone switchboard has always been the central core of the organization telecommunications system. With the convergence of computing and communications the importance of that central core has increased. The decision to purchase a new PABX is a complex one. Alan Horne, writing in *Communications Management* (Feb 1985), outlined the following general areas for consideration:

(a)   Network configuration: Is the PABX to be linked to a local area network and, if so, what will be the consequent demands upon it?
(b)   Number of extensions and external lines, including plans for future growth.
(c)   Integrated voice and data: how many terminals are required to handle both data and voice traffic? To what services should they be connected?
(d)   Applications.
(e)   Traffic handling capacity.
(f)   Reliability.
(g)   Potential suppliers of PABX.

Potential purchasers may decide to delegate at least some of the decision making to a suitable consultancy organization.

In terms of newer features offered by PABXs the following list outlines some of the more important new features not covered in the earlier section on telephones. These are:

(a)   *Queuing.* When all lines to the company are engaged the PABX will automatically store incoming calls in a queue, until a line becomes available. The same facility can also be used for internal calls.
(b)   *Transfer-on-busy/no reply.* This ensures that incoming calls to an individual go to the next most appropriate member of staff if that individual is engaged or does not answer. Set procedures like these can be programmed into the PABX, and after that no manual intervention is required to maintain the facility. This type of facility is particularly useful in a sales office, for example.
(c)   *Hunting groups.* This involves segregating extensions into groups according to their functions. For example, sales,

accounts or warehousing can each contain a number of different extensions. A call will be passed by any engaged extension in a group.

(d) *Conferencing.* This is the facility for two-way conversations between a number of people in the organization and between them and an outside caller.

(e) *Moving extensions.* The facility to move to a new office in a building and take the extension number with you. This gets rid of the need to memorize new extension numbers and the need to update internal directories.

(f) *Alarm call.* If you are due at an important meeting you can program your telephone to remind you by ringing at the relevant time.

For many small businesses some of the above facilities may be inappropriate, either because they are not needed or because the company cannot justify a centralized switchboard with an operator. New 'key systems' may provide an answer to the latter problem. These allow everyone in the office to act as a receptionist – each telephone acting as a small switchboard in its own right. This gives flexibility that centralized systems do not have. Key systems are modular in design and, hence, can be expanded at will. A typical network will have ten to twenty telephones attached to a central box. Because they use microprocessors they rarely malfunction. They are modest in price (and prices are currently falling).

Modems and acoustic couplers

Modems and acoustic couplers provide part of the mechanism by which computers may communicate via the public telephone network, or via private leased telephone lines. Communication between computer devices is a form of data transmission, and the telephone network (the Public Switched Telephone Network or PSTN) is the most commonly used medium for data transmission, both nationally and internationally.

The telephone network was designed for human voice transmission and operates in an analogue form where constantly varying electrical currents represent the different speech forms. In contrast, data from computers are presented in a digital form (based on 'off' and 'on' signals only). Hence, if computer data are to travel down the PSTN lines, they must be converted from a digital form into an analogue form. This process is known as modulation. To make use of the information transmitted, the receiving computer must have the process reversed and the signal has therefore to be demodulated back to its original digital form. A modem (a contraction of modulator/demodulator) is the device which interfaces between the computer and the telephone system at each end and carries out these functions.

There are two basic types of modem – that known simply as a modem and that known as an acoustic coupler. The former, strictly a hard-wired modem (often labelled direct-connect), links the computer directly into the PSTN via the standard British Telecom phone socket. That is, it does not involve the use of the telephone handset as part of the linkage. (An additional lead may link the modem to an adjacent desk telephone, which is only required for the initial dialling of the number of the remote computer.) 'Intelligent' modems are now available which include automatic dialling, answering and disconnection features, and thus do not require the adjacent desk telephone. Most hard-wired modems are mains powered and, hence, require sites that have mains electricity and a PSTN socket.

Acoustic couplers are modems that enable a computer to access PSTN lines through the standard telephone handset. Physically they consist of a small box with two rubber cups into which the telephone receiver is fixed. A lead connects the coupler to the computer. The operator dials the remote computer as for a normal call and waits for a reply tone from the answering computer. When this tone is received, the operator quickly places the handset within the coupler's rubber caps and the connection is established. Acoustic couplers suffer from more transmission errors than hard-wired modems as extraneous noise in the vicinity of their operation may be picked up. Their advantage is their portability and they are therefore popular with users of portable computers, who may wish to communicate data from a hotel bedroom, or public telephone, for example.

Summary

This chapter has sought to provide a brief survey of some of the newer telecommunications facilities that are now available, and may be of use to the small to medium-sized organization. It has concentrated on current capabilities relevant to the business use, with little emphasis on technical details. Prices have not generally been included because in many cases they are likely to vary considerably with time due to continuing cost-reducing innovations.

5 Information and expertise

Suppose that, having read the previous chapter, the reader decides that organizational efficiency would be substantially increased if he/she were to have a cellular mobile telephone installed in his/her company car. The subsequent decision making is unlikely to be so complex as to require the employment of a communications consultant. A decision will have to be made as to which network to join (Cellnet or Vodafone), and then it is simply a matter of deciding upon which mobile telephone to purchase or rent, balancing cost against sophistication and reliability. Such decisions may be based upon literature from the service/telephone suppliers, supplemented by the reading of articles in such magazines as *Communications Management*, if the manager feels that this is necessary. The likelihood of a serious error in the decision making due to lack of expert advice is not high, and the costs of any such error are relatively low.

In contrast, the decision to purchase a new PABX system with the capability for incorporating it into a proposed local area network may well require advice from someone expert in the field. Similarly, the decision to review line management communications procedures in a medium-sized organization may also call for the assistance of a consultant trained in this area.

For any problem or planned change there exists a range of options from pure DIY by the manager to the delegation of the whole task to outside experts. The decision as to which option to choose can only be made by the manager concerned. Factors to consider are the level of in-house expertise, the costs of failure, the consultancy costs and the simplicity or complexity of the problem. In this chapter some of the possible sources of outside expertise will be outlined. It is hoped that this list of sources, combined with the individual manager's knowledge of the problem, will provide a satisfactory basis for initial decision making.

The sources of information/expertise to be examined are:

(a)   Sales staff and advertising literature.
(b)   Books.
(c)   Magazines, journals and other periodicals.
(d)   Conferences, courses and exhibitions.
(e)   Consultants.

In looking at these sources and at communications auditing in general it is worth noting that there are two main dimensions to be considered in organizational communication systems. Firstly, there are people who communicate and whom we might wish to motivate more efficiently by improving communication procedures. Secondly, there are the pieces of equipment by which we communicate, the telephones, the microcomputers, the telex, etc. It is true to say that many of the sources of information/expertise to be discussed below are largely directed towards one or the other of these dimensions, i.e. towards people or towards equipment.

Sales staff and advertising literature

On this topic there are two relevant and ancient sayings that provide guidance. The first, based on the Trojan horse experience, is: 'Beware Greeks bearing gifts'. The second, also of an equine nature, is 'Never look a gift horse in the mouth'.

The objectives of both the advertising literature of suppliers of communications equipment and their sales staff are the same, i.e. to sell the company's product. It does not follow that this product is the one best suited to your needs. Generally sales staff and advertising literature do not make statements like 'No, I'm afraid our system does not provide all the facilities you want, what you need is the one provided by our main competitor', or 'Yes, our product does just what you want and it's only £10,000 more than all the other similar products on the market'. On the other hand, literature about suppliers' products can be very useful for providing information on what is available. It is often a good starting point when looking at a new facility or replacing equipment, especially as such information is free. It is obviously necessary to obtain information from a number of suppliers when considering your communications (or wider) objectives. The suppliers' sales staff are a more interactive and intelligent potential source of expertise at the later stages of the decision making process, when the purchaser has already gathered some preliminary facts.

Books

If one is concerned with capabilities and facilities provided by communications equipment, books suffer from the disadvantage of rapidly becoming dated. Therefore, if you wish to discover the current state of the art or usage of teletext, for example, magazines are a more suitable source.

There are other aspects of communications auditing, however, where relevant books do not date so rapidly. Some have already been mentioned specifically at the end of Chapter 3. Besides these, good books on communications in organizations from a management studies perspective can give useful background. The majority of these are American, but much of what they say is relevant to managers generally. These books typically deal with topics such as leadership, communication in groups, management structures and their impact on communication, and the human communication process itself. They provide a useful theoretical base from which to examine the motivational aspect of communications systems, prior to analysis or the initiation of change. Managers seeking to improve their own personal communications ability may also find relevant sections in this type of book. Some books deal specifically with this latter topic alone; although again they tend to be written by American authors.

The area of strategy and planning for communications is covered in the book *Corporate Communications Networks* by J.E. Lane (1984). This work is concerned with the capabilities of newer communication systems now available. It aims to provide guidelines for planners involved in creating strategies for the development of communications within their own organizations. Chapter headings indicate the main topics covered:

- Where are we now?
- The need to communicate
- The next five years
- Options for the future
- Integrated voice and data in the office
- Network strategy for the eighties
- Elements of a communications strategy
- A strategic plan

Finally, those wishing to discover more about the state of communications auditing in the UK in the 1980s will find this topic covered in *Communications Audits: A UK survey* by A. Booth (1986).

Magazines, journals and other periodicals

A number of publications are available that deal with telecommunications equipment from the business user end, and allow readers to keep up to date with the latest developments. Perhaps the most specific in this context is *Communications Management*, which is published monthly. All aspects of modern business communications are covered in articles and product advertising. There are periodic review articles, e.g. 'PABX Update: The Technology and Benefits' and frequent case study descriptions of how companies are using the new systems. *Communications Management* is aimed at UK-based telecommunications and data communications managers. It is therefore angled more to larger companies than small, and frequently requires more technical background knowledge of its readers than many general managers are likely to have.

Less specific, but covering similar areas, are the monthly publications *Business Equipment Digest*, and *Business Computing and Communications*. A more specific publication is the bi-monthly *Telelink*, which covers videotex and telecomputing, public and private viewdata, electronic mail, bulletin boards, teleshopping and telesoftware.

Other useful services for current awareness of communications equipment are some of the weekly and daily newspapers. On any one day, taken at random, the chances of finding an article about telecommunications are low, but relevant articles are appearing with increasing regularity in the following: *Times, Financial Times,*

Sunday Times, Daily Telegraph, Sunday Telegraph, Observer, Guardian. Relevant articles may tend to appear on a particular day of the week, e.g. *Guardian* 'computer' day is usually Thursday.

Looking towards the motivational side of good organizational communications, it is less easy to find relevant information in periodicals than for equipment. Management publications of a more general nature are the most likely candidates for current awareness in this area. For example, *Management Today* and *Personnel Management* deal with this type of topic. Perhaps the most specific publication for the manager interested in employee communications is the magazine of The Industrial Society, called, appropriately enough, *Industrial Society.* The objective of the Industrial Society is to promote the fullest involvement of people in their work and, hence, their magazine often features organizational communications as a topic. The Work Research Unit which is part of ACAS (Advisory, Conciliation and Arbitration Service) is also interested in this area and regularly produces an information service news sheet.

Conferences, courses and exhibitions

Regular scanning of the journals mentioned above will give some idea of conferences, courses or exhibitions likely to be of interest to readers. All three may occur regularly, or on a more *ad hoc* basis, dependent upon user demand. For example, 'Communications 86' is one of an annual series of exhibitions, which also incorporates a conference on some aspect of communications technology of current interest. Conferences, courses and exhibitions are organized by various types of body. The most important factor to investigate prior to attendance is the topic and its relevance to you, both in terms of subject and bias. The financial cost of courses is such that full details are needed in advance to ensure that the experience will be cost-effective. A two-day course on corporate communications could cover anything from a technical discussion of data transmission systems to the value of worker participation in management. Frequently professional and trade associations provide a source of information on courses oriented to a particular type of business. The Industrial Society regularly runs courses related to the human resource management side of communications. Finally, consultants are likely to organize, or know of, relevant courses in their area of specialization.

Consultants

The sections above have briefly indicated some of the sources of information available to managers to increase their knowledge of communications issues. The information they provide may be useful enough to help the individual make a decision in this area without other outside assistance. They may, on the other hand, alert the manager to the fact that the decisions involved are too complex to be handled on an internal DIY basis.

Increasingly, over the last few years, organizations have been turning to consultants rather than employing specialists on a permanent basis. Smaller organizations, however, sometimes reject out of hand the idea of employing consultants when they become aware that fees per day tend to start from a minimum of £200. This is a shortsighted approach. The cost of not taking expert advice is often much higher. This may, for example, involve paying too much for an unsuitable PABX, or even eventual corporate bankruptcy because of the wrong strategy decisions being taken by an ill-informed board of directors.

The biggest problem for companies who have not used consultants before is deciding upon a suitable consultancy firm. Also the range of communications issues that might call for consultancy is wide. Clearly, it is necessary to obtain the most appropriate expertise for the specific problem. One possible starting point is the *Directory of Management Consultants in the UK* (an annual publication) which is compiled and published by Alan Armstrong and Associates Ltd. This directory lists over 1000 consultancies ranging from individual one-person consultancies to multinational organizations employing hundreds of consultants. Besides an alphabetical listing which gives details of each consultancy, there is a regional index for organizations seeking a locally-based consultant. Also there is an index of key areas of specialization which contains both wide categories such as 'Personnel management', and more specific ones such as 'Communications', 'Employee attitudes' and 'Telecommunications'.

Some of the information in this directory is provided by the Management Consultancy Information Service, a body which is supported by the CBI. The MCIS is also a central source of information on management consultants in the UK. Its function is to help those considering using consultants to select firms and individuals whose experience and background will make them most effective within the client organization. The service provided is free, confidential and may be used without obligation. It operates from:

38 Blenheim Avenue
Gants Hill
Ilford
Essex 1G2 6JQ

Telephone No: 01–554–4695.

Another source of information on the professional services that management consultants can provide is the Management Consultants Professional Register. This is jointly operated by the two professional organizations for management consultancy in the UK, namely the Institute of Management Consultants (IMC) and the Management Consultants Association (MCA). The Management Consultants Professional Register is at:

23/24 Cromwell Place
London SW7 2GL

Telephone No: 01–584–6655.

Organizations which have access to the Prestel Viewdata system can obtain information on the above register by looking up the heading 'Consultants' on the Prestel A–Z index. Information is provided on the scope of the service offered by the register, how it works and how to obtain further information.

By using the above sources the potential client may gain access to the majority of management consultants in the UK. However, there are organizations carrying out communications auditing which are not accessible in this way. Some are management consultants not registered with the above services, others are simply not management consultants. Even some management consultants who list communications as one of their main areas of expertise do not carry out communications audits. Also organizations specializing in the telecommunications side of communications auditing tend to be more accessible through telecommunication/computing avenues.

As a consequence of research carried out in 1985 the author was able to find a total of 92 organizations and individuals who carried out communications auditing activities for their clients. These are:

Actionline Business Consultants Ltd
Alec Crombie & Associates
Annan Impey Morrish
Arthur Young
Aubrey Wilson Associates
Binder Hamlyn
BIS Applied Systems
Brian R. Clark
Business Planning and Development
Business Research (Systems) Limited
Butler Cox & Partners Limited
C.S.P. International
Campion Willcox and Associates
Cargill Attwood International
Central Computer Agency
Challenger Communications Consultants Ltd
Charles Barker Communications
Clifford & Company
Cockman, Copeman & Partners Limited
Collins Consultants
Collinson Grant Consultants Ltd
Communications Studies and Planning Ltd
Communication Improvements Ltd
Communications and Employee Relations Training Ltd
Communication Audit
Coopers and Lybrand Associates
Coverdale Organisation Limited
Cripps, Sears & Associates
Daley McGivern Associates
Deloitte Haskins and Sells
Denis Guy & Partners
Dorset Management Training Centre
E.J. Fancett Management Consultant
EMAS Business Consultants
Employment Relations Associates
EOSYS
Epic Industrial Communications
Eric Mitchell
Ernst & Whinney Management Consultants
F International Ltd

Glendenning Associates International
Gordon Coote
Graeme Robertson Associates
Handley-Walker Company Limited
Hay-MSL Management Consultants Group Ltd
Inbucon International Consultants
Industrial Management and Engineering Company
Industrial Energy Cost (Telecoms) Ltd
Industrial Market Research Limited
Industrial Society
Irene Knightley Associates
Jack Harvey and Partners
Knight Wendling
Leo Kramer International
Leon Simons
Logica UK Ltd
Lopex
Management Development Services (N.I.) Ltd
Maple Communications
Market & Opinion Research International
Media Bond Ltd
Metra Consulting Group Ltd
Modern Materials Management Limited
National Computing Centre
O.D. (Management Consultancy) Ltd
Organisation Dynamics Ltd
Pactel
Peat Marwick
Personnel Relations Limited
Price Waterhouse Associates
Professional Personnel Consultants Limited
R. Warwick Dobson
Roy Talbot & Associates Limited
Salford University Industrial Centre Ltd
Samia Jazaery
Sheppard Moscow & Associates Limited
Space Planning Services Limited
Speechpower
Stoy Harwood Associates
Telecom User Reports Ltd
Telecommunication Consultancy Services
Teleplan Informatics Ltd

Touche Ross & Co.
Towers, Perrin, Forster and Crosby
Turnkey Management International
Unilever Computer Services Ltd
Urwick Dynamics
Urwick Management Centre
Verax Limited
Vivian Stokes
Walpole Training & Development Ltd
Workplace Consultants Ltd

This list should be a suitable starting point for organizations seeking some sort of communications audit. It is necessary to remember, however, that not all these consultancies carry out all the activities that may be classified under the umbrella heading of 'communications audits'. Some have a human resource management perspective and are heavily oriented towards communications auditing as a tool to improve motivation of the workforce. Some are primarily concerned with the hardware of telecommunications. Some are very specialized and may just deal with single-item measures, such as call logging. Others see the communications audit as a tool to be used in larger organizational restructuring projects.

Finally, it is worth noting one trend that is occurring as a consequence of the convergence of telecommunications and computing. This is the increase in consultancy projects related to the development of overall IT (Information Technology) strategies for client organizations. Having an IT strategy is one way to overcome the inconsistencies and inefficiencies of piecemeal purchasing of computer and communication facilities. The development of such a strategy should ensure that the growth of computer/communications systems within the organization is consistent with predefined corporate objectives. Communications auditing may be seen as a central component of developing such a strategy regardless of whether it is carried out in-house or with the aid of consultancies. Organizations contemplating employing a consultant to help them develop an IT strategy will find a useful source of information in a survey carried out by *Business Computing and Communications* and the Institute of Administrative Management. The survey asked leading consultancy firms about their particular approaches to IT strategy development. Findings are summarized in the May 1986 issue of *Business Computing and Communications*.

6 A systems approach

In looking at communications auditing techniques and modern communications equipment in earlier chapters, the various techniques and equipment have been largely presented to the reader in discrete specific 'parcels'. This has been done both to identify the component parts of communications auditing, and to aid understanding. In real organizational life the problems that we face are not so discretely packaged. They are frequently complex and complicated. Often the real problem is not the one that appears at first inspection; alternatively, a 'simple' communications problem may later be found to contain many other issues.

In this chapter, two problem-solving methodologies will be described that should be useful to managers dealing with more complex or difficult communications issues. Both these methodologies are known as 'systems' methodologies or approaches. The first, the 'hard' systems approach, should be of value to managers employing consultants to investigate communications issues that relate mainly to telecommunications and computer equipment. The second, the 'soft' systems approach, should be of value to managers wishing to attempt their own problem solving, especially in relation to human resource management.

The systems perspective is useful in increasing understanding of the functioning of an organization (amongst other things). The basic concept is that we may look at organizations as systems. Further, the particular organization may be seen as a subsystem of a larger system, e.g. the UK manufacturing system. Organizations

also contain subsystems; internal departments, paper work systems, purchasing systems for example, may be seen in this way.
In this context a system may be defined as follows:

1 An assembly of parts is connected together in an organized way.
2 The parts are affected by being in the system, and they and the system are changed if they leave it.
3 The assembly of parts does something.
4 The assembly has been identified as of special interest to someone.

According to the third part of the above definition, the system 'does something' and one way to look at the essence of any system is to see what it does. In this context, a system can be represented as something that takes an input from its environment, processes or transforms that input in some way, and then 'puts out' the transformed product to the environment.

The organizational internal telephone system can be seen as a system within this type of definition:

1 The parts are the telephones connected by wires and the central exchange.
2 If the parts are removed (i.e. disconnected) they will not function and people dialling those extensions will not be able to get through.
3 The assembly of parts allows individuals in different offices to speak to each other.
4 The system is of special interest to someone (especially when it breaks down).

Another example is provided by the research centre where the author is currently employed. This organization may itself be seen as an information-generating or processing system:

1 Some of the parts of the system are its employees and they are connected in an organized way, partly determined by the management hierarchy.
2 The staff are affected by being in the system and both they and the system change when they leave it. For example, if a member of staff leaves the research centre, the centre's capacity falls and the individual loses a source of income.

3   This system processes and generates information: taking in information by various means and disseminating new or transformed information via books, journal articles and lectures, for example.
4   The research centre is of interest to someone, e.g. its funding body or the purchaser of its outputs.

The 'hard' systems approach

Research carried out by Booth (1986) showed that one way to classify communications audits carried out for clients by consultants is along a Technology orientation v People orientation dimension. Two particular projects mentioned by the consultants interviewed that were highly technology-oriented were:

1   'A telecoms audit looking at the current configuration of a particular communications network in relation to cost/efficiency, and examining whether different configurations would be cheaper/more efficient.'
2   Analysing the current and projected telephone facilities for a central London firm of solicitors in order to recommend which type of PABX they should purchase to satisfy their needs for the next ten years.

Any small to medium-sized organization might want to look at such issues. However, it is unlikely that they could do this efficiently without bringing in outside expertise. The 'hard' systems methodology to be described below will not allow managers to carry out such work for themselves; but it will provide background knowledge that will be helpful in ensuring that any consultants employed by the company on such a project is under the control of the manager concerned, rather than vice versa. In order to do this, it is necessary to describe the 'hard' systems methodology in outline only, so that the manager can have a generally informed view of the problem-solving process without trying to become expert in that particular field. Readers wishing for a more detailed knowledge of the hard systems methodology, so that they can apply it themselves, will need more specialist texts, such as *Systems Thinking, Systems Practice* by Peter Checkland (1981). Alternatively, the Open University provides a number of useful courses on systems approaches to management and the study of organizations.

In describing the 'hard' systems approach, the author does not suggest that any consultants employed are necessarily likely to use this approach themselves. They may do so, as the approach has its roots in engineering and related areas. If they do not, the manager concerned will obtain just as much benefit from carrying out a preliminary analysis of the problem, or area of concern, using this methodology.

The 'hard' systems approach allows an individual or team to tackle more effectively problems that are poorly structured or complex. Such problems are frequently described as 'messy problems'. To do this one goes through a number of stages:

● Build up a comprehensive picture of the situation and the issues involved in it.
● Set objectives for the change which accurately reflect the decision-makers' concerns.
● Design a range of options for alternative strategies which meet the objectives.
● Manage the choice between alternative options.
● Develop a strategy for actually implementing the changes.

The underlying logic of the approach is therefore one of thinking through rigorously the implications of a range of possible options in relation to a set of explicit, relevant criteria. The latter component is the reason for the label 'hard' systems approach, as the criteria are normally of a quantifiable nature. The variables quantified may be anything of a suitable nature relevant to the particular problem, e.g.

● Cost in money
● Percentage of incoming calls not answered
● Probability of equipment failure
● Increase/decrease in productivity.

In order to illustrate this hard systems methodology in relation to communications auditing, it will be useful to describe a simple scenario where such an approach might be valuable.

You are a senior manager with responsibility for sales in a medium-sized consumer product manufacturer. The Managing Director calls you into his office to discuss a project he has in mind that he wants you to handle with the aid of an outside consultant, if necessary. Following a seminar that he attended, organized by the local branch of the British Institute of Management, the MD is keen on improving the company's overall efficiency. He is also aware that because of the recessionary climate it is proving more and more difficult for the company to maintain sales volume and profitability. He feels that, rather than looking for changes of a structural nature that will affect the whole company, one specific area should be tackled, namely that of communications with customers. After some discussion, you and he decide that one crucial question should be examined: 'What new equipment or changes in procedures should we invest in so that we can communicate more effectively with our customers?'

Step 1: system description

In this stage we aim to define where we are now, before looking at where we want to be. Therefore it is necessary to identify and describe the problem to be solved, and the existing system and its environment and behaviour. This stage, being the first one, is more likely to shape the project as a whole more than any other. Partly because of this, there are a number of sub-activities to be considered which help in the system description.

The first of these is 'problem perception'. Problems do not normally exist in any objective absolute sense. They exist because of the subjective perceptions of individuals or groups. Two important 'problem perceptions' (in this example) are yours, as sales manager, and that of your MD, who can be described as the 'problem owner'. It is important to explore early on whether these two perceptions are the same and, if not, how they differ. They may differ because the MD has the responsibility for the whole company whilst yours is only for the sales function.

The second activity is known as 'detection' and involves looking for the aspects of the problem that can be viewed as systems, using the definition given earlier in the chapter. There may be parts of a situation that do not have a systems element, but in this particular case we can identify a number of relevant systems and subsystems, for example:

- The manufacturing system
- The delivery system
- The ordering system
- The invoice processing system
- The (internal and external) telephone systems.

In the third activity, 'separation', the various systems, sub-systems and non-systemic components are sorted out and related to each other. The environment and system boundary should be defined, and decisions made as to which are the subsystems. For example, the telephone system may be seen as a subsystem (or component) of both the ordering system and the invoice processing system (if it is used for the placing of orders and the chasing up of overdue payments).

In the fourth activity, 'selection', some systems are chosen as more important and given more detailed inspection. This stage might include the telephone system, if customers were having difficulty in getting through to the sales department to place orders, for example. It might involve the manufacturing system if ways were to be examined of speeding up delivery times.

The earlier stages when combined lead to the fifth activity, namely 'detailed description' of the existing situation, which includes some type of diagrammatic representation of the situation.

Step 2: Identification of objectives and constraints

In this step we look at where we would ideally like to be. This step helps to clarify thinking on what is hoped for, and brings into the open any disagreements. We can define an objective as a 'desired outcome' and a constraint as a 'condition which must not be violated'. Generally objectives relate to things we have control of (within the system boundary), whereas constraints are normally beyond our control (and associated with matters in the system's environment). We can also set objectives at different levels, since they frequently have a hierarchical nature. For example, having a successful sales conference in Paris is a higher-order objective than arranging for the collection of the air tickets (that are necessary for you to fly to Paris to run the sales conference).

In the context of the example we have been using, some of the possible objectives will have been discussed at the meeting between the MD and the Sales Manager. Part of the hierarchy of objectives that might follow from further discussions is given in Figure 6.1.

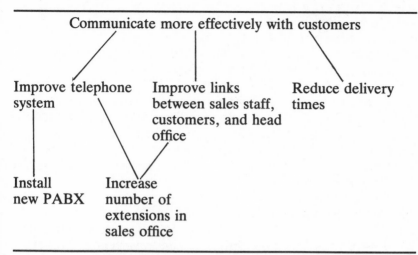

Figure 6.1 Possible hierarchy of objectives in improving communications

In this situation, one obvious constraint is financial: as profits are not high at present, there may be little money to spend on improvements. A less obvious, but equally real, constraint might be the ways things have previously been done within the company. More radical solutions might not be acceptable, even if they can prove to be cost effective, e.g. letting sales staff negotiate reduced prices with customers on their own sites, without consulting head office.

Step 3: Formulation of measures of performance

This is an essential part of the 'hard' systems approach, which emphasizes the need to have measurable means of assessing the effectiveness of any potential solution. Measures are chosen at this stage for determining which option comes closest to meeting the chosen objectives.

Looking at the objective 'improve telephone system', we first choose a measure of performance: for example, the time it takes for a customer telephoning the company to be connected to an appropriate member of the sales staff. (Clearly speedy connection in this context is good, as it makes it easier for the customer to place an order by telephone.) This is therefore an appropriate measure of performance with regard to this objective. It is then

107

necessary to set a target level of achievement in relation to that measure; in this example it might be: 'less than one minute for *all* incoming calls from customers'. The final stage of this step is to set a target time by which the level of achievement is to be attained.

Looking at one of the other objectives, e.g. 'improve links between sales staff, customers and head office', a suitable measure of performance is perhaps not so obvious, and it may be necessary to split the objective up. Looking at links between sales staff and customers alone, one 'closed' objective incorporating a measure of performance could be 'every customer who orders more than £x of goods per annum to be visited by a sales representative on average once per month'.

Step 4: Generation of options (routes to objectives)

In this step we produce as many different ways as possible, at least initially, to achieve the required objectives. Creative generation of a wide range of routes is followed by a narrowing down to feasible options. There are various techniques such as 'brainstorming' that can be used in the creative component. For the objective 'improve telephone system', we might produce the following ideas, of varying feasibility:

- Buy new PABX that has a 'hunting group' facility
- Increase number of extensions
- Employ more telephone operators
- Hire a private line to each customer
- Increase number of outside lines
- Demand that British Telecom improves the quality of its service nationwide
- Invest in a freefone facility for all callers
- Install newer telephones.

For the objective of improving links between sales staff and customers the list of options might include:

- Increase number of sales representatives
- Improve training of sales representatives
- Increase sales representatives' pay
- Increase amount of expenses allowed (so that representatives could treat customers to lunches, etc.)

- Provide all staff representatives with portable computers (and modems)
- Hire a private box for the use of customers at the local football or cricket club or theatre.
- Provide representatives with cellular car telephones.

It is important at this stage to include a number of silly or obviously unfeasible ideas as they may lead on to innovative but practical solutions.

Step 5: Model construction

Broadly speaking, a model is any set of organized assumptions about a particular aspect of the world and the way it works. Models are used in the context of the 'hard' systems methodology to test likely outcomes of the options being considered in terms of the measures of performance. In long-term large projects complex computer models are used. In the context of communications auditing the latter type of model may be left to the consultant. The client applying the 'hard' systems methodology may safely restrict himself/herself to fairly simple common-sense arithmetic techniques to predict the behaviour of the system when following particular routes to objectives.

Looking at the area of improving links between sales representatives and customers, some assumptions that may be part of a model have been stated or implied overtly, for example: 'Frequency of visits by representatives affects sales to the customer'.

Examining this further, we could tighten up this assumption. If our representative called every day then the customer would soon get tired of him. We might also feel that if the representative calls less than once every two months, then the customer would feel neglected and would perhaps decide to look for another supplier. Therefore an equation summarizing the assumption is

$S = f(n)$
where $6 < n < 26$

S = sales per annum in £
n = number of visit per year

($f(\ )$ stands for a function of; $6 < n < 26$ means that n should fall between 6 and 26, i.e. a minimum of once every 2 months and a maximum of once every 2 weeks)

Developing this further we might suggest the following set of assumptions:

Volume of sales obtained from any customer is a function of

(a) Frequency of seeing representative
(b) Quality of interaction between sales representative and customer
(c) Quality of the product
(d) Price of product
(e) Size of customer.

With more thought and knowledge of the field, further items could be added and each one developed in the manner of item (a). Some items in the model will be beyond the control of the problem owner and, whilst they cannot be ignored, they are less important in the problem-solving process.

The discussion above has looked at a general model related to sales volume. If now we deal with the more specific issue of the factors that determine how many visits a representative might be expected to make to major customers, we can obtain a model that allows us to evaluate options in this area. The following set of assumptions is presented as relevant for purposes of illustration (sales managers and others may question this model and should be able to develop a better one):

Number of visits to major customers is a function of:

(a) workload per representative
(b) time spent at head office
(c) time spent travelling
(d) motivation of sales representative
(e) geographical spread of customers
(f) quality of interaction between customer and representative
(g) size of order obtained from customer.

Each of these factors can be broken down further as necessary, e.g. time spent travelling is related to:

(a) Time spent at head office
(b) Efficiency of communications with head office
(c) Quality of representative's company car, etc.

Step 6: Evaluation

Assuming that the model is credible (i.e. it mimics the behaviour of the real world fairly well), the evaluation step is fairly simple. An evaluation matrix may be used to compare the relative or absolute values of the different options against the measure of performance.

In the earlier section on measures of performance, the example chosen was that of visits per month by the representative. However, we have also noted that cost is a constraint. In real situations one measure of performance would be inadequate. For this situation, therefore, we may add cost as a measure of performance (as we do not have unlimited funds), and motivation of sales staff (as if this falls too low they will not make many sales, even if they do visit their customers more frequently).

Now it is simply a matter of looking at each option with regard to the three measures. As we already know the number of visits per month at present, we can probably work out quite accurately the number of visits that could be achieved by an increase of 50 per cent in the number of sales staff. The matter of motivation is more difficult to quantify and model. However, it should be possible to compare options with regard to motivation on the basis of: (A) will probably be best in terms of motivation; (C) will be the second best, etc. Using a scale of 1–n (where 1 is the most preferred option and n the least preferred), a matrix may be compiled that allows a total to be obtained for each option.

To obtain the figures in the matrix, it is simply necessary to look at each of the options and feed them into the model whilst looking for their effectiveness with regard to the particular measure of performance being examined. Thus in Figure 6.2, based on the models the author is using (partially illustrated above), increasing the number of sales representatives is the most effective method of maximizing the number of visits. However, it has the highest cost and its postulated effect on motivation is about average for options.

Assuming all measures of performance to have similar weightings, cellular telephones for the representatives is the best option, followed by portable computers and improved training.

| | Measure of performance | | | |
Routes to objectives (options)	No. of visits (maximize)	Cost (minimize)	Motivation (maximize)	Total
(a) Increase sales reps	1	7	4	12
(b) Improve training	4	4	1	9
(c) Increase pay	6	6	4	16
(d) Increase expenses	7	5	4	16
(e) Portable computers	3	3	2	8
(f) Private box	5	2	7	14
(g) Cellular phones	2	1	3	6

Figure 6.2   Matrix on maximizing number of visits

Step 7: Choice of routes to objectives

An issue that may be raised at this stage, although it should not be restricted to it, is that of iteration. This is an important aspect of all systems methodologies. At any stage in the methodology, increased understanding of the system might call for a repetition of the process which takes account of the new knowledge. For example, one concept associated with the quantity of visits to customers by sales staff is the quality of such visits. Having looked at the area of relations between customers and sales staff relative to frequency of visits, we may want to re-evaluate our findings by also including the efficiency of the visits. To do this, a suitable measure of performance would be the size of the order obtained per visit. The models used would need to be developed further, and possibly new ones included. A second such iteration is likely to produce a better solution than the first, or at least a greater understanding of the problem.

Step 8: Implementation

This step is carried out following a suitable number of iterations. It obviously follows from any problem-solving analysis, not just a 'hard' systems one. The use of the 'hard' systems methodology should ensure that implementation is at least based upon clear objectives and thinking, and is no more painful than it needs to be.

The 'hard' systems methodology has proved to be a valuable

problem-solving approach in many areas. Managers planning to employ a consultant would be advised to work through the steps above in relation to the problem area they plan to have studied. By doing so before approaching the consultant they will start with a clearer understanding of issues involved. This will help them stay in touch with the problem the consultant is addressing for them and will maximize the chances of a cost-effective solution.

The 'soft' systems methodology

The methodology that will briefly be described in this section is the Checkland 'soft' systems approach. Checkland developed it because he saw the need for a way of handling those problems in organizations which were not clearly defined. We are rarely able, when faced with a substantial problem at work, to say in advance, 'Ah, this is a communications problem', or 'Yes, this is a leadership question'. The Checkland methodology allows us to take a complex unstructured situation and find important themes within it. Sometimes one of the themes may relate to communications, at other times it may not. The case study used here to illustrate the methodology is not primarily concerned with communications, although it contains communications elements. The main purpose of this section is to provide a general problem-solving approach that is useful in complex situations, whether or not they apparently contain communications components at the outset.

The case study is based upon problems being faced by Mary, the organizational employee who provided the author with the relevant information. The case illustrates the type of 'messy' problem that the Checkland methodology is designed to handle and it describes a real-life situation in the mid-1980s.

The Warren House project provides services and support for physically handicapped people and their families. The project provides support both in Warren House on a day-care basis and in the wider community.

Mary and Kate are home-care supervisors in charge of a team of home-care staff. Their team provides help in a variety of ways. They may look after a handicapped person in Warren House; they may take them on trips;

they may provide regular help with housework and other chores to hard-pressed families. In times of family crisis they may take over a large part of the responsibility for looking after the handicapped member altogether.

Mary and Kate organize the team so that someone is available to give the required support when it is needed. The team consists of eight women who are largely well-motivated and adaptable to working unsocial hours, often at short notice. Mary and Kate are also respons-ible for running a 'sitting' service for Warren House (sitters look after the handicapped person so that their parents, for example, can go out to the pictures, etc.). This service is not free, unlike the other services, but is subsidized, in that the payments made by people using the service are not enough to cover the payments to the sitters, who are paid according to the number of hours sat. Some members of the home-care team do this type of sitting on top of their normal work, but there are not enough of them to meet the demand. Most of the sitting is done by others not employed at Warren House, who 'sit' on a casual basis.

The demand for the sitting service and the home-care service is very variable from week to week, but has been growing steadily since the start of the project. Because of the variable demand, Mary and Kate have periods when they have more work than their staff can handle and others when there is not enough work. Each woman is paid to work 18½ hours per week and they fit their working weeks together according to the needs of the job.

The project was funded initially by a local charity with support from the government, who paid workers under the MSC community programme, but later the local authority agreed to provide some stable funding for the project for three years. A number of the staff (some of them home-care) are still funded by the MSC com-munity programme and thus have only one-year con-tracts. The project is now one year into its new funding with two years to go before it needs to apply for a new grant from the local authority.

The head of the project is Jack; Mary and Kate report directly to him although when he is away another supervisor, on the same level as Kate and Mary, deputizes for him. Jack is funded by another source and on a fixed two-year contract and he is now halfway through it.

Since the project started, it has increased its service to the handicapped consistently, especially the service offered by the home-care section. This success has had several implications for Mary and Kate's job. It has meant an increase in their staff to eight and so, when there is a slack week, more effort is required in finding things for them to do. Also administrative duties are increasing, which means Mary has to spend more time at her desk. This prevents her (and Kate) from paying regular visits to the families concerned to check up that they are getting all the help they need. It also prevents her from establishing links with potential new clients.

One reason for the increased desk work is the success of the sitting service. More and more sits are arranged every month as demand increases. This means that Mary and Kate have to spend more time telephoning sitters to make arrangements, which is a particularly lengthy process if the sitter is required at short notice. Also, as demand increases so extra sitters have to be recruited. The financial side of the sitting service raises two kinds of problem. Firstly, Mary and Kate have to spend more time each month working out the payments to the sitters and sending cheques out to them. Secondly, they have to keep asking the project manager for increases in subsidy as demand grows. (The payment made by users of the service is always less than the sum paid to the sitters.)

Another potential problem concerns relations with colleagues. Mary gets on very well with Jack, Kate and most of her subordinates. However, Pamela, the present deputy, is demanding that she should have line management authority over Mary and Kate. Mary feels strongly that although Pamela is very good at other parts of her job, she is a poor manager and hence a change in this direction would be a total disaster! Mary is currently trying to convince Jack that the system of line management should stay as it is, because it works well.

Finally, Mary has just realized that home care is now

at the limit of its capacity. Having taken on some clients recently who will require a regular long-term commitment of hours it is apparent that there is no slack in the system to deal with increases of demand, no matter how short or temporary. Mary is faced with the need to refuse to provide support to families for the first time in the history of the home-care service.

The first stage of the methodology is the unstructured problem situation (as described in the case study above, for example). It simply acknowledges the perception of a problem situation.

The second stage involves the analysis of the situation. At the end of this stage, a 'rich picture' should have been produced and a number of themes identified.

In the third stage, the methodology leaves the real-life situation and goes into an abstract world of systems thinking where relevant systems are identified with the themes. These systems are defined by their 'root definitions'.

This abstract development is then taken further in the fourth stage when 'conceptual models' of the systems are developed.

In the fifth stage, the theoretical conceptual models are compared with the real world situation described in stage two to see if the comparison generates any ideas for change and improvement.

This is followed by a debate on feasible and desirable changes in the sixth stage, before the final stage of implementation of changes which are intended to resolve problems identified at the beginning of the process.

The whole purpose of the methodology is to compare the actual situation with a theoretically based system (or systems) so that fundamental rather than superficial changes may be achieved. Terms like 'root definition', etc., which are part of the methodology, may appear unnecessary jargon at first, but their value will be perceived as the approach is described in more detail below.

Stage 1: The unstructured problem situation

This is described in the case study itself above and is taken from the viewpoint of Mary.

Stage 2: Analysis

This stage is not about defining a problem! An attempt to do this so early in the process would be inappropriately restrictive in terms of generating innovative solutions.
Analysis looks at:

(a) Structure components such as: physical layout, hierarchy, reporting structure and patterns of communication.
(b) Process components, i.e. basic activities such as: planning, doing, monitoring performance and taking action when things are not going as planned.
(c) Climate: The relationship between structure and process.

Analysis can be a lengthy process and, as a minimum, it should answer the following questions in relation to the problem situation.

● What resources are deployed, in what operational processes, under what planning procedures, within what structure, in what environment and wider systems, by whom?
● How is this resource deployment monitored and controlled?

One of the ways to work towards an appropriate level of analysis is in the generation of a 'rich picture'. A rich picture is a graphic device that seeks to represent as many aspects of the situation as possible. It may be thought of as a cartoon, an economical way of representing a lot of information in a small space. It is usually backed by a key or supplementary explanation in a text form. Generally, rich pictures should:

● be holistic
● incorporate structures and processes
● summarize and communicate the situation
● not impose a systems view on the situation.

A rich picture of the case situation, with supplementary notes, is presented in Figure 6.3.

The main components of the picture are the clients, the project manager and the three types of service provided by the project.

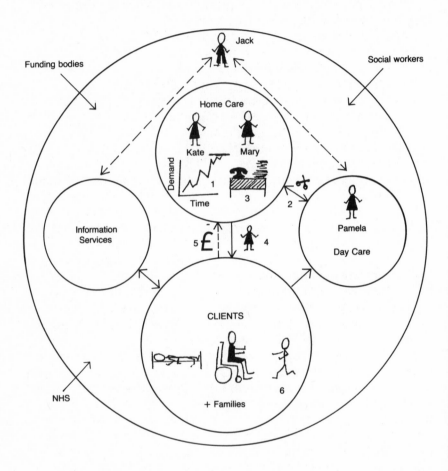

Figure 6.3   Rich picture of problem situation

1 indicates the rising, but erratic, demand on the services of the home-care and sitting services and the fact that capacity has been reached.

2 the crossed swords show the (potential) conflict between home care and the head of the day care service.

3 shows the rising paperwork load in home care.

4 indicates that home care workers actually go out to the homes of customers (a main process of the system).

5 means that money is paid by clients for part of this service.

6 indicates that the clients have various types of handicap and that their families are also included in the service.

Other factors shown are that the NHS, the funding charity and social workers come into the picture. The arrows indicate flows of money, people or information between the components indicated.

From the rich picture, and analysis prior to its drafting, we should be able to draw a number of problem themes. Potential candidates in this situation are:

(a)   The increased demand for home-care services
(b)   The increase in administration associated with (a).
(c)   The conflict between Pamela and Mary that could occur if Pamela was promoted.

It is important to stress at this stage that in dealing with complex issues like those brought up in this case there are no obvious correct answers. The problem themes defined above are those perceived by one analyst (the author) in a case study that looks at the issues primarily from the point of view of the home-care service. Another analyst might come up with different themes, or the same analyst might identify different themes as further information becomes available. Like the 'hard' systems methodology, Checkland's approach is iterative. Also if the problem situation had been described by the project manager, for example, different themes are likely to have surfaced due to his perspective differing from that of home care.

The final part of the analysis stage is to name relevant systems for each of the problem themes. In the example (c) above, the author feels that there is not an appropriate system, as the problem appears to be a 'one-off' from the point of view of the home-care service. (If the analysis was being done for the project manager, it would be worth following this theme and looking at it within the context of a staff development system or an organizational development system.) There are, however, systems that might usefully be linked with (a) and (b) in the view of the author. These are:

(a) A priority determining system
(b) An administration minimization system.

Stage 3: Root definition of relevant systems

The two systems that seemed relevant in the previous stage, following our analysis of the situation, now need to be developed further. It should be stressed that we are not talking here about systems that already exist within the organization, or even systems that should be 'installed' in the organization. We are dealing with theoretical systems that appear relevant in some way to a central aspect of the situation. We are looking for what might be termed logic-based systems.

The root definition of a system is a statement that tells you what the system does at its most fundamental level. The objective of the root definition is to provide insight into the system. As such, there is no correct 'root definition', but some attempts provide better insight than others. One also has to decide upon the level of generality of any root definition. Three possibilities for system (a) are:

● A system to determine priorities in the allocation of home-care staff to the clients of the service that balances client needs with home-care efficiency.
● A system to determine priorities in the allocation of home-care staff to clients that is consistent with the objectives of the Warren House project.
● A system to determine priorities in the allocation of home-care staff that maximizes potential support for the physically handicapped people in the local area.

The first root definition is the most specific to the home-care service itself, and would be appropriate in looking at a system from the point of view of the home-care supervisors. The second root definition, being more general, is perhaps most appropriate to the viewpoint of the project manager. The third and most general root definition takes account of the fact that the Warren House project is only one agency providing services in the local area. Consequently, a priority system in this context might consider those services that have no other local 'suppliers' as the ones with the highest priority.

A root definition concerned with the administration problem might be:

> A system to ensure that administration carried out by home-care supervisors is maintained at the minimum necessary level.

Stage 4: Conceptual model building

This starts from the root definition and asks: 'What activities would have to be in a system that met the requirements of the root definition?' The aim is to include all the activities implied from the definition (not from the real world problem situation) and build them into a model developed from the root definition using logic alone. The model displays the activities expressed as verbs and connected by logic-based arrows. For example, taking the first root definition from the previous stage, namely: 'A system to determine priorities in the allocation of home-care staff to clients that balances client needs with home-care efficiency', activities defined by verbs are 'determine (priorities)' 'allocation' and 'balance'. It is necessary logically to know: (1) client needs; (2) home-care efficiency. Part of the conceptual model is shown in Figure 6.4.

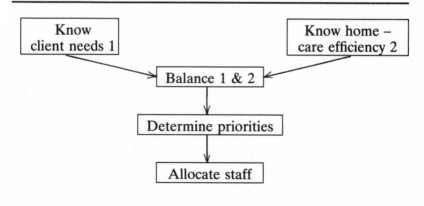

Figure 6.4   Part of conceptual model

The next step is to consider what other activities are implied logically by these starting activities and put them into the model. Thus, 'know client needs' implies some procedures for obtaining information on clients' needs from the various sources available. 'Know home-care efficiency' implies considering measures of efficiency and factors that affect efficiency. When these factors are incorporated the model develops into Figure 6.5.

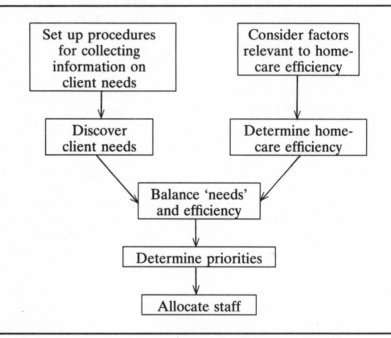

Figure 6.5   The next stage in the conceptual model

Two questions arise at this stage, namely, when do we stop adding components to the model, and what about feedback? Concerning the first, we could consider activities implied by the revised model again and carry on making a more and more complex model. There is no simple answer to the question of when to stop; it is a matter of judgement, bearing in mind that the objective of developing the model is to increase understanding by the analyst. A useful role of thumb is that any model (in the first iteration), should contain 7 + 2 activities.

The second question, that of feedback, relates to the fact that 'successful' systems tend to have feedback mechanisms within them. It is probably *logically* valid to draw a feedback line from the 'allocate staff' box to the 'consider factors relevant to home-care efficiency' box, as there is a logical link between the two. One might also argue that the allocation of staff can feed back to 'set up procedures for collecting information on client needs'; as when staff have been allocated to a client to perform a particular task they can provide information on client needs following that interaction. This would *not* be appropriate, however, as it implied looking at *how* something might be done rather than *what* is logically implied as a part of the system. A first pass conceptual model for this root definition is shown in Figure 6.6.

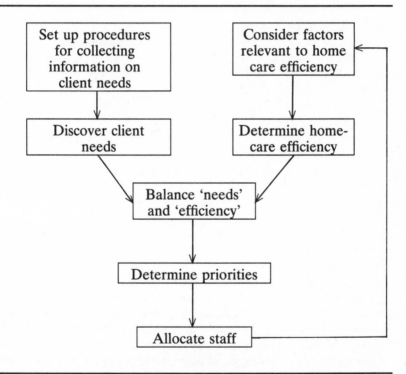

Figure 6.6 **Conceptual model based on the root definition: 'A system to determine priorities in the allocation of home-care staff to clients of the service that balances client need with home-care efficiency.'**

Stage 5: Comparison of conceptual model with real world situation

This is done to reveal possible changes which could 'improve' the problem situation. Remember that the conceptual model is there to help structured problem solving and not to define what 'ought' to be happening in the real world. Conceptual models should provide insight to those concerned with the problem. Even when they succeed in this purpose, they tend to be rather antiseptic or detached from the humanity and history of the real-life situation. They should therefore be viewed as a tool, rather than a specification.

Looking at the conceptual model in Figure 6.6 and comparing it with the problem situation can raise issues for debate with those involved in the problem in various ways. One approach is to say: given that the conceptual model implies *what* activities are called for, let us look at how, if at all, the necessary activities are embodied in the real world. Sufficient detail is not given in the case described earlier to do this with any precision, but it is possible to identify important issues such as:

1   What are the measures of home-care efficiency that organizational members or clients acknowledge as appropriate?
2   How is information about client needs collected at present?
3   What factors regarding efficiency of the service are taken into account at present when allocating staff?
4   How would staff respond to a more rigorous system of allocation?
5   How would clients respond to changes in the ways they were given help by home care?

Stage 6: Debate on feasible and desirable changes

The issues identified are then debated in relation to their feasibility and desirability by those concerned with the problem situation. In this case, this would include the project manager, the home-care supervisors, the home-care staff and some clients of the service. Depending upon the implications of changes proposed, it may also be necessary to include the day-care supervisor, the funding charity, the information services supervisor and some outside bodies, such as social workers.

Following such discussion, proposals for change are made. For example, following debate on issue 2 in the previous stage, the proposal may arise: 'That each time a member of the home-care service visits a client to give support, the member of staff should write a brief visit report indicating any change of circumstances that might affect client needs'.

Stage 7: Implementation of recommended changes

This stage follows logically from the others. However, it does not follow automatically from the first iteration of the methodology. It is likely that, as proposals are debated, an increased understanding of the problem situation will call for at least a second iteration where the analysis is more detailed or takes a different perspective. Alternatively, iteration may be needed to develop the conceptual model further to provide for more detailed consideration of the logistics of change.

Conclusions

The two systems methodologies that have been described in this chapter represent the author's view of a 'hard' approach and a 'soft' approach respectively. They are intended to be useful to the reader who seeks to deal with complex issues in an organization, whether with the aid of outside assistance or not. In reality 'soft' problems contain 'hard' elements that may be measured, and 'hard' problems are always embedded in 'softer' issues. With some problems it is apparent that one or the other approach is called for. When problems arise that are not so easily classified, a first iteration of both methodologies is worthwhile.

Bibliography and reading list

Booth, A., *Communications Audits: A UK Survey*, Taylor Graham, London, 1986.

Checkland, P., *Systems Thinking, Systems Practice*, John Wiley, Chichester, 1981.

Directory of Management Consultants in the UK, Alan Armstrong and Associates Ltd, London (annual publication).

Emanuel, M., *Inside Organizational Communication*, Longman, New York, 1985.

Goldhaber, G.M. and Rogers, D.P., *Auditing Organizational Communication Systems: The ICA Communication Audit*, Kendall/Hunt, Dubuque, 1979.

Gunning, R., *The Technique of Clear Writing*, McGraw-Hill, New York, 1952.

Hoinville, G. and Jowell, R., *Survey Research Practice*, Heinemann, London, 1978.

Horne, A., 'Choosing a PABX', *Communications Management*, February 1985, pp.37–8.

Lane, J.E., *Corporate Communications Networks*, NCC Publications, Manchester, 1984.

Odiorne, G.S., 'An Application of the Communications Audit', *Personnel Psychology,* Vol. 7, 1954, pp. 235–43.

Open University – Course Units for Systems Courses: T241, T243, T301. The Open University, Milton Keynes (various dates).

Index